GCSE Drama

DNA

by Dennis Kelly

DNA is pretty twisted. It has murder and cruelty, guilt and betrayal...
and a really tense scene involving a waffle*.

Luckily, this CGP book straightens out everything you need to know
about the play for GCSE Drama — from context and themes
to character performance and design.

We've also included plenty of practice questions to sharpen your skills, plus
a whole section on how to write brilliant answers in the exam. Amazing!

*Make the most of it — it's the only waffle you'll find in this book.

The Play Guide

CONTENTS

CONTENTS

Section Four — Staging and Design

Section Five — Close Analysis

Section Six — Exam Advice

The Characters in 'DNA'
'DNA' Cartoon

Published by CGP

Editors:
Claire Boulter
Andy Cashmore
Emma Cleasby
Alex Fairer
Sophie Herring
Jack Tooth

Contributor:
Mike Vogler

With thanks to Louise McEvoy, Katya Parkes and Helen Jeffery for the proofreading.
With thanks to Emily Smith for the copyright research.

Acknowledgements:

_With thanks to Hull Truck Theatre for permission to use the image on the cover
and the images on pages 3, 4, 5, 27, 30, 37, 38, 40, 48, 62 & 63._

With thanks to Alamy for permission to use the image on page 1.

_With thanks to ArenaPAL for permission to use the images on pages 2, 5, 6, 11,
16, 18, 19, 21, 23, 29, 35, 39, 43, 49, 50, 57, 59, 60 & 61._

With thanks to Photostage for permission to use the images on pages 3, 4, 8, 10, 13, 17, 32, 36, 46, 52, 56 & 58.

_Images on pages 3, 9, 28, 34, 47 & 53 from the Next Big Thing Festival 2014,
Auckland Theatre Company, New Zealand. Photo: Michael Smith._

With thanks to Rex Features for permission to use the image on page 12.

_With thanks to Arno Declair for permission to use the images on pages 22, 26, 31,
33, 44, 45 & 51, from the Deutsches Theater 2010 production of DNA._

ISBN: 978 1 78294 963 3
Printed by Elanders Ltd, Newcastle upon Tyne.
Clipart from Corel®

Based on the classic CGP style created by Richard Parsons.

Introduction to 'DNA'

'DNA' was written by Dennis Kelly

1) _DNA_ was written in <u>2007</u> and is set in the <u>early 21st century</u>.

2) It's one of <u>many</u> plays written by <u>Dennis Kelly</u>, a British playwright (see p.12).

3) The play includes <u>tragic</u> and <u>comic</u> elements — it has <u>serious themes</u> and an <u>unhappy ending</u>, but there are moments which can be played <u>humorously</u> to <u>relieve tension</u>.

4) It also has aspects of a genre called <u>in-yer-face theatre</u> (see p.16). For example, it features <u>violent</u> moments that may be <u>distressing</u> to watch.

> ### _DNA on Stage_
> Directors need to know the <u>key features</u> of the play before they produce it on <u>stage</u>. Aspects of the play such as its <u>context</u> and <u>genres</u> might influence how it is <u>performed</u> and <u>designed</u>.

It's a play about responsibility and bullying

DNA is about a <u>group of teenagers</u> who think they've killed one of their schoolmates and try to <u>cover up</u> his 'murder'. Many of the play's themes focus on how the group <u>behave</u> and the <u>consequences</u> of their actions:

1) **Responsibility** — The characters <u>don't</u> take responsibility for their <u>actions</u> or for their <u>treatment</u> of others. As a result, Adam <u>dies</u> and the postman is <u>wrongly arrested</u>.

2) **Bullying** — The play shows the <u>destructive</u> consequences of bullying and how it can be used to <u>hurt</u> and <u>manipulate</u> people. It shows how it can <u>affect bullies</u> too, e.g. some characters feel guilty.

3) **Power** — Kelly suggests that <u>power</u> brings out the <u>worst</u> in people and can cause them to <u>act immorally</u>.

4) **Identity** — The characters face a <u>struggle</u> between trying to <u>fit in</u> with the group while acting in a way that is <u>morally right</u>. They <u>suppress</u> their <u>individual identities</u> in order to <u>protect</u> the group <u>as a whole</u>.

> ### _DNA on Stage_
> <u>Directors</u> should consider the <u>themes</u> that they want to emphasise when making <u>production decisions</u>. For example, a director might choose to highlight the lack of individual identity in the group by using <u>costume design</u> to dress everyone the same.

The play reflected British society at the time

See p.6-7 for more on the social context of the play.

1) The play's characters and events are all <u>fictional</u>, but Kelly uses them to <u>raise questions</u> about <u>real social issues</u> that existed in <u>early 21st-century Britain</u>.

- There was a strong sense that <u>anti-social behaviour</u> amongst <u>young people</u> was getting <u>worse</u>. This was part of what was labelled '<u>Broken Britain</u>' — a British society in which people acted <u>for themselves</u> rather than in a <u>socially responsible</u> way.

- An increase in <u>terrorism</u> caused <u>anxiety</u> and led to stricter <u>surveillance laws</u>. These laws were intended to protect the public, but some people saw them as an <u>invasion of privacy</u>.

2) The action takes place in <u>generic locations</u>, and the play isn't set in a named town or city — the play's events could be happening <u>anywhere</u> in Britain. This makes it <u>easier</u> for the audience to engage with the play and the <u>questions</u> it raises about <u>British society</u>.

Introduction to 'DNA'

The play is still relevant today

As *DNA* was written in the <u>early 21st century</u>, a lot of its themes and messages are still <u>relevant today</u>:

- There's still <u>anxiety</u> around <u>terrorism</u> and the <u>surveillance measures</u> used to protect the public against it — it's <u>unclear</u> whether it's okay to limit the rights of individuals to protect society.
- The play tackles other issues that exist in today's society — <u>anti-social behaviour</u> and <u>bullying</u> are still problems.
- Some of the play's themes are <u>universal</u> — *DNA* explores ideas such as <u>power</u> and <u>identity</u> that would be recognisable to <u>any audience</u> in <u>any time period</u>.

Directing *DNA*

Kelly's <u>note</u> at the start of the play states that the names and genders of the characters can be <u>changed</u>. This gives directors more freedom to explore the questions raised by the play in their own way.

Its dramatic features appeal to audiences

See Section Two for more on the play's dramatic features and the techniques that Kelly uses.

DNA is one of Kelly's most popular plays. This is partly due to the <u>dramatic features</u> which make it <u>entertaining</u>:

1) The play contains a mixture of <u>dark</u> and <u>comedic</u> moments. This makes it <u>enjoyable</u> to watch, as the comedy provides light relief from the tense and serious nature of the play.

2) The play is <u>simple</u> and doesn't have a lot of different <u>plot lines</u>. This makes it easy for the audience to <u>follow</u> the <u>main action</u>.

3) It's also <u>short</u> and the action is <u>fast-paced</u>, which keeps the audience <u>gripped</u>. By the end of Act Two, the group have already <u>covered up a murder</u> and let an <u>innocent person</u> take the blame.

4) The play is open to <u>interpretation</u>, so every production <u>varies</u> in the way it's <u>performed</u> and <u>designed</u>. This means that even audiences who are familiar with the play will find <u>new meaning</u> in each production.

'DNA' has been performed numerous times

There's more information about past productions on p.12-13.

1) *DNA* was originally written to be performed by <u>youth theatre groups</u> as part of the <u>2007</u> National Theatre Connections project. Kelly and other playwrights were asked to write plays for young people to perform, which were then staged in <u>different productions</u> across the UK.

2) The first <u>professional production</u> of *DNA* came in <u>2008</u> at the Cottesloe Theatre in London (part of the National Theatre).

3) The play <u>toured nationally</u> in England for the first time when it was performed by the Hull Truck Theatre Company in <u>2012</u>.

4) *DNA* first appeared on the <u>West End</u> in <u>2016</u> when it was performed by the National Youth Theatre. The production was a <u>sell-out</u> and it was staged for a third time in <u>2018</u>.

5) The play has also been <u>performed abroad</u> by professional theatre companies in Germany, New Zealand and America — its <u>universal themes</u> make it <u>appealing</u> to audiences all over the world.

The National Youth Theatre production in 2018 used young actors.

Who's Who in 'DNA'

Leah...

...is a moral character who worries about the group's actions. She is insecure and seeks Phil's attention.

Phil...

...is the group's leader for most of the play. He's a quiet, emotionless and manipulative teenager.

Cathy...

...is violent and remorseless about Adam's 'death'. She helps to kill Adam after he reappears.

Adam...

...is bullied by the group and thought to be dead. He turns out to be alive, but Phil has him killed.

John Tate...

...starts as the group's leader, but his authority is weak. He leaves the group early in the play.

Richard...

...seems unhappy about the cover-up, but he goes along with it. He challenged John Tate's leadership in the past.

Danny...

...is a selfish character who is more worried about becoming a dentist than Adam's well-being.

Jan and Mark...

...act as narrators who explain what's happening. They're always together and help in the cover-up.

Brian...

...is the weakest group member. He's bullied into covering up Adam's 'death' and he suffers a mental breakdown as a result.

Lou...

...worries about the group getting caught. She follows whoever is in charge.

Introduction

Plot Summary

'DNA'... what happens when?

Here's a little recap of the main events of *DNA*. It's a good idea to learn what happens when, so that you can consider how elements of performance and design might change as the plot progresses.

Act One — Phil comes up with a way to cover up Adam's 'death'

- On "*A Street*", Mark tells Jan that someone is dead, but it isn't clear who (it turns out to be Adam).

- Leah talks to Phil in "*A Field*" about her insecurities and tries to get his attention — Phil doesn't respond.

- In "*A Wood*", Danny and Lou panic about Adam's 'death'. John Tate bans the word 'dead' in an attempt to maintain control of the group, but he struggles to assert his authority. John Tate and Richard clash over who should be in charge, but John gets the others on his side.

- Jan and Mark meet the others in the wood and describe Adam's accident to Leah and Phil. The group dared Adam to walk on a grille over a mineshaft, before throwing stones at him until he fell.

- Phil comes up with the idea of framing a non-existent postman for kidnapping Adam. He tells Cathy and Mark to get DNA from a stranger and Brian to give the police a fake description.

- Later in "*A Field*", Leah talks to Phil about bonobos, chimps and humans. She threatens to kill herself, but Phil ignores her.

Act Two — the cover-up gets an innocent postman arrested

- On "*A Street*", Jan and Mark express concern that someone isn't going somewhere (it's later revealed that Brian is refusing to go to the police).

- Meanwhile in "*A Field*", Leah shows Phil a pet that she has killed, but he is unmoved. She says that everyone is happier since Adam's 'death', but that John Tate won't leave his room.

- Danny and Lou explain to the group in "*A Wood*" that a man has been arrested for Adam's disappearance. It turns out that Cathy and Mark collected DNA from a postman matching the description given to the police.

- Jan and Mark bring Brian to the group. He refuses to falsely identify the postman to the police, but gives in after Phil threatens him.

- Back in "*A Field*", Leah talks to Phil about déjà vu and repeating mistakes. She asks Phil if he believes that it's possible to change the world. He says no.

Introduction

Plot Summary

Act Three — Adam returns weeks after disappearing

- On *"A Street"*, Jan and Mark <u>panic</u> because Cathy found someone in the woods (it turns out to be <u>Adam</u>).

- Leah threatens Phil in *"A Field"* by <u>pretending to leave</u>, but he <u>doesn't react</u>. She reminds Phil that everyone is <u>happier</u> thanks to him — apart from <u>Brian</u>, <u>John Tate</u> and the <u>framed postman</u>.

- The group gather in *"A Wood"* to see <u>Adam</u>, including Brian who has had a <u>mental breakdown</u>. Leah thinks it's <u>good</u> that Adam is <u>alive</u>, but others are <u>worried</u> his return will <u>expose</u> their cover-up as a <u>lie</u>.

- Adam, who is <u>injured</u> and <u>traumatised</u> after his fall, tells the group about <u>escaping from the hole</u> and <u>living in a hedge</u>.

© Helen Murray / ArenaPAL

- Phil asks Adam if he wants to live in his hedge or return home, but <u>manipulates</u> him into <u>going back</u> to the hedge.

- Leah <u>protests</u> that Adam needs <u>help</u>. Instead, Phil instructs Cathy and Brian to find Adam and <u>suffocate</u> him using a <u>plastic bag</u> to stop the group's secret coming out.

- Afterwards in *"A Field"*, Phil <u>offers</u> Leah a sweet, but she <u>storms off</u>. Phil <u>calls after</u> her, but she <u>doesn't come back</u>.

Act Four — the cover-up is successful, but Leah leaves the group

- Jan and Mark talk on *"A Street"* about someone <u>leaving</u> and <u>moving schools</u> without saying <u>goodbye</u> (it's implied that this is <u>Leah</u>).

- Richard <u>takes Leah's place</u> in *"A Field"* alongside Phil, who has clearly been affected by <u>Leah's departure</u>.

© Hull Truck Theatre

- Richard tells Phil what's happened to the other characters, but he doesn't mention <u>Leah</u>, <u>Adam</u> or the <u>framed postman</u>.

- Cathy is now <u>in charge</u> of the group, and she's <u>more violent</u> than John Tate or Phil. Lou has become her <u>best friend</u>.

- John Tate has <u>found God</u>, Danny <u>hates</u> work experience at a dentist's, Brian might be sent to a <u>psychiatric hospital</u> and Jan and Mark are <u>shoplifters</u>.

- Richard asks when Phil will come back to the group, but Phil is <u>silent</u>.

Not knowing the play is like trying to get away with murder...

It's definitely a good idea to get to grips with basics like the plot and characters before you start studying the play in more detail. Once you've got a feel for what's going on and who's doing what, get cracking on Section One. Alternatively, you can take a look at the cartoon at the back of the book to make sure you really understand the plot.

Early 21st-Century Britain

I reckon you know a lot about life in the early 21st century — call it a hunch — so you may already know all about the 21st-century issues the play references. But in case you don't, here are two lovely pages on them...

The threat of terrorism was making people anxious

1) *DNA* was written in 2007, when the growing threat of <u>terrorism</u> in Britain was causing <u>anxiety</u>. Two major terror attacks that contributed to this fear were the <u>September 11th 2001</u> attacks in the USA and the London Bombings on <u>7th July 2005</u>. In Leah's first monologue, she describes the "brutal <u>terror</u>" that everyone lives in. This fear links the play to the wide-scale fear of <u>terrorist groups</u> in the 21st century.

Effect on the Audience

Leah's monologue creates a <u>foreboding mood</u> for the audience, even <u>before</u> the group's horrifying actions become clear.

Set Design

A designer could place <u>CCTV cameras</u> at the sides of the stage. In the opening scene in the street, Jan or Mark could <u>spray paint</u> on the lenses to <u>foreshadow</u> the group's decision to <u>cover up</u> Adam's death.

2) To increase <u>security</u>, <u>stricter surveillance</u> measures were introduced by the government — for example, more <u>CCTV cameras</u> were installed in public spaces. In the play, the wood provides a secluded space where the group can discuss their plans <u>unobserved</u> by CCTV or other surveillance equipment.

3) Extra security measures were intended to <u>protect</u> the public, but they also created concern because they <u>reduced</u> the amount of <u>freedom</u> and <u>privacy</u> individual people had. The play touches on this concern — through their desire for <u>self-protection</u>, the group gets the postman <u>arrested</u>, while Cathy, Danny and Mark <u>invade</u> Adam's <u>privacy</u> when they enter his home and take his belongings.

Young people were a political issue

1) There was growing media <u>representation</u> of <u>anti-social</u> behaviour amongst young people, including underage drinking, shoplifting and gang violence. The characters in the play discuss taking part in these activities.

2) This created <u>distrust</u> of young people — some older people saw them as a <u>threat</u>.

Costume Design

The characters could wear <u>hoodies</u> — this would make them seem more <u>anonymous</u> and <u>threatening</u> to the audience.

© Elliott Franks/ArenaPAL

3) There was a concern that young people acted like this because of a <u>poor education system</u>. Some people thought that schools weren't teaching young people the <u>skills</u> they needed to get a job, so they resorted to anti-social behaviour. In the play, most of the characters show no interest in <u>school</u> or their <u>futures</u> — only Danny cares about his future career as a dentist.

4) The media and some politicians used terms like '<u>Broken Society</u>' and '<u>Broken Britain</u>' to describe the idea of a culture where people acted for <u>themselves</u> rather than in a socially responsible way. This idea is reflected in the behaviour of the characters — they commit a terrible act and choose to <u>lie</u> rather than take responsibility for their actions.

Set Design

A designer could scatter the stage with <u>litter</u> and old <u>shopping trollies</u> — this would hint that <u>social irresponsibility</u> is an issue in the play, linking the performance to the theme of a 'Broken Society'.

Early 21st-Century Britain

Technology meant young people spent more time online

1) Technology became more advanced, and mobile phones and social media were everyday things. People no longer needed to go out to see friends.

2) This led to an increase in social isolation, with some young people feeling lonely and detached. This is reflected in the play — Leah says "I haven't got friends". Even though she is part of a group, she feels alone.

3) The lack of real friendships in the play may help to explain why the characters act so callously towards one another.

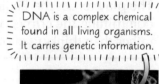

Proxemics

Leah could stand some distance apart from other characters to mirror her isolation.

Effect on the Audience

The characters don't use technology in the play and rarely mention it. This makes the time period in which the play is set less prominent, which may mean its appeal to audiences endures.

4) Violent content on the internet and in video games became easier to access. Research suggested that some young people became desensitised to violence as a result. Some characters, like Cathy and Phil, use or threaten to use violence frequently — this could suggest they have been desensitised.

DNA changed our understanding of the world

1) The early 21st century brought scientific advances in DNA research.

2) The majority of human DNA was sequenced for the first time in the Human Genome Project. This meant scientists could compare human DNA with other animals to help us understand our ancestry. In the play, Leah talks about how chimpanzees were thought to be our closest living relative, until science showed that we were more closely related to bonobos.

3) Forensic science, which is used to analyse scientific evidence such as fingerprints and DNA from crime scenes, became more efficient and was used more frequently. It became a part of standard procedure and was viewed as a reliable way to gather evidence.

4) Knowledge about DNA, forensic science and their applications became widespread. This knowledge allows the characters in DNA to come up with a plan to cover up Adam's 'death'.

DNA is a complex chemical found in all living organisms. It carries genetic information.

DNA normally forms a double helix, like this.

People became more concerned about the environment

1) Knowledge about the potential impacts of global warming became more widespread, and people became more worried. There were also concerns that the environment could be damaged by the improper disposal of nuclear waste.

2) Leah's Act Two monologue suggests that she is anxious about these environmental issues — she mentions global warming and nuclear waste. She seems to view life on Earth as fragile, hinting that she fears future environmental devastation.

Set Design

During Leah's monologue, an image of a large red sun could be projected onto a backdrop to highlight environmental issues. The sun's dominance would make Leah's anxieties more real to the audience.

I thought this was Drama, not Biology...

You'll need to consider the social, historical and cultural contexts of DNA in your exam — there are lots of design and staging choices that may be influenced by the things happening when the play was written.

Guilt and Responsibility

You know that feeling when you have an exam coming up, but instead of revising you're hanging around in the wood getting away with murder? That's called guilt. Take responsibility and crack on with some revision.

The characters fail to take responsibility for their actions

1) The group is <u>responsible</u> for <u>bullying Adam</u> and bringing about <u>the fall</u> in which they believe he died. The characters <u>know</u> that they've done something awful, but they <u>won't accept</u> responsibility:

> • <u>No one</u> contacts the police or tries to <u>get help</u> for Adam — the characters' first instinct is to meet as a <u>group</u> to decide what to do.
> • When Brian says that they should "<u>tell someone</u>", John Tate immediately <u>suppresses</u> him.
> • Individual members of the group try to <u>deny</u> or <u>justify</u> their parts in what happened to Adam — Jan says she "went home" before Adam's fall, and Mark claims that Adam was "laughing".

2) Any <u>individual</u> in the group could tell the authorities what they've done, but doing so would incriminate <u>everyone</u>. The group has to act as <u>one</u> to protect itself, so individual opinions are disregarded.

Effect on the Audience

The play forces the audience to question who is ultimately <u>responsible</u> for Adam's death — the <u>group</u> for committing the crime, or <u>society</u> for creating an environment where people often look out for themselves rather than thinking of others. This may make the <u>audience</u> question their attitude towards others in real life.

The characters lie to avoid responsibility

1) The first <u>lie</u> of the play — the plan to cover up Adam's 'death' — is intended to <u>shift</u> the responsibility for Adam's disappearance <u>away</u> from the group.

2) Phil gives <u>everyone</u> in the group a job, apart from himself and Leah. This means everyone is <u>responsible</u> for the <u>cover-up</u>, which gives them all an <u>incentive</u> to keep quiet.

3) The lie <u>escalates</u> when the postman is arrested. Phil forces Brian to falsely identify the suspect — this passes the responsibility for Adam's disappearance on to the <u>postman</u>.

4) Some characters seem to <u>believe</u> the lies — <u>Lou</u> talks about "the man who kidnapped Adam" as if it <u>really happened</u>, and Leah has to remind her that it's a lie. This suggests that lies are <u>stronger</u> than the truth.

© Donald Cooper/ photostage

Effect on the Audience

Adam's 'death' (and subsequent murder) and the postman's innocence are easily <u>concealed</u>. This highlights how <u>fragile</u> the <u>truth</u> is, which may unnerve the audience.

DNA evidence is central to the group's lies

For more on DNA and forensic science, see p. 7.

1) The group's **knowledge** of DNA and forensic analysis allows them to **manipulate evidence** — this frees them from responsibility for Adam's disappearance.

2) **DNA evidence** is generally seen as **reliable** — this works in the group's favour. The DNA evidence they **plant** on the jumper is taken as **proof** of the postman's guilt, which means the group are out of danger.

Character Performance — Phil

In Act One, an actor playing Phil could use a **confident tone** when he talks about the bin bag being a "DNA nightmare". This would emphasise that he's **knowledgeable** about forensic science.

Guilt and Responsibility

Some characters feel guilty...

See Section Three for more on how the characters handle guilt.

Guilt affects the characters in <u>different</u> ways. It generally makes them <u>unhappier</u>:

- Brian wants to tell the truth but is <u>forced</u> to lie. His guilt results in a <u>mental breakdown</u>.
- John Tate <u>withdraws</u> from the group early in the play and isn't seen on stage after Act One. In Act Two, Leah says he's "lost it", and in Act Four Richard says he's "found god" — this may suggest that he's trying to <u>make amends</u> for his part in bullying Adam.
- Danny's guilt <u>ruins</u> his hopes of becoming a dentist — his <u>fear</u> that he might "fall in" to a patient's mouth suggests that Adam's fall into the mineshaft has affected him deeply.
- Leah's <u>inability</u> to stop Phil from killing Adam causes her to <u>leave</u> Phil and the group without saying goodbye, and to change schools.

Directing *DNA*

Kelly gives no indication of whether Leah is <u>happier</u> after she leaves. A director could have her <u>on stage</u> in the last scene, sitting away from Phil and Richard with her back to them. This would allow the audience to <u>see</u> whether Leah still <u>feels guilty</u> after leaving the group.

Performance Skills

Actors need to think about <u>how guilty</u> the character they are playing might feel at <u>different</u> points in the play, and how they could use a range of <u>physical</u> and <u>vocal skills</u> to convey this.

... while others don't seem to feel any guilt

© Michael Smith/ Auckland Theatre Company

1) Some <u>characters</u> go through the play without showing <u>any remorse</u> for Adam's 'death' or the postman's arrest:

- Cathy <u>enjoys</u> the drama that comes from Adam's disappearance — she finds it "<u>exciting</u>" and focuses on whether the media will pay her for her story.
- Jan and Mark seem <u>less affected</u> by events than other characters — they take up <u>shoplifting</u> at the end of the play, and the similarity of their duologue in Act Four to their other duologues suggests that their lives have <u>carried on</u> as before.

Physical Skills

In the final scene, Phil could <u>hunch</u> over and <u>stare</u> blankly into the distance to hint that he regrets his actions.

2) It's hard to judge how guilty Phil feels. He arranges to have Adam murdered without showing any sign of <u>guilt</u>, but his behaviour in the final scene could be interpreted as <u>regret</u>. However, it's <u>unclear</u> whether that's because he feels guilty or because Leah has gone.

REVISION TASK

My least favourite kind of holiday — a guilt trip...

Imagine that you are Brian, and that you want to tell the truth about Adam's disappearance. Write a diary entry explaining your thoughts directly after Act One ("A Wood"). Write about:

1) What you think will happen if you tell someone the truth.
2) Whether or not you will tell the group you want to reveal the truth and why.

Putting yourself in the same situation as the characters who feel guilty could give you ideas on how to direct or perform these characters.

Power and Group Dynamics

Knowing how the characters feel about each other will help you understand how they should interact on stage. Sadly, the characters in *DNA* don't seem the type to have sleepovers and late night heart-to-hearts.

Power shifts between characters throughout the play

1) There are three leaders of the group during the play. As the play progresses, more ruthless and controlling characters take on the role of leader:

© Donald Cooper/ photostage

- The first leader is John Tate, whose authority is shaky. He is insecure in his leadership, and people feel able to challenge him.
- The second leader is Phil, who maintains control for most of the play. He rules by threats and manipulation.
- The final leader is Cathy, who is the most violent — Richard says that she "cut a first year's finger off". Having her in control of the group as the play ends creates an ominous mood.

Effect on the Audience

The leaders become more powerful as the play progresses. This makes the audience worry what the group will do next.

2) As more violent characters take charge, the rest of the group become more timid and less likely to question the leader's choices. The audience sees this during Phil's time as leader, when everyone who could prevent Adam's death seems powerless to do so.

3) The increasingly tyrannical leaders drive the group to commit more brutal acts — they progress from bullying to murder.

Characters who aren't respected are bullied

Peer pressure also plays a role in the group. Brian is uneasy about the cover-up, but goes along with it because the others pressure him.

Weaker characters become victims of the group:

1) Adam is the main victim — the other characters abuse him physically and mentally. Mark and Jan suggest that he allowed himself to be bullied because he was "trying to be part of" the group — they take advantage of his desperation to fit in.

2) Brian is intimidated by stronger characters — he tries to stand up for what he believes in, but Phil easily threatens and manipulates him into doing what he wants. Other characters largely ignore him, apart from Cathy who bullies him.

Performance Skills

Characters could look away when Brian speaks or talk over him to show their lack of respect for him.

Bullying is used to gain power

1) Stronger characters bully weaker characters as a way of gaining and maintaining power.

2) There are three types of bullying in the play:

- Physical — characters are physically harmed, e.g. Cathy slaps Brian.
- Verbal — characters are threatened with words, e.g. Cathy tells Brian to shut up or he'll "be dead".
- Emotional — characters are intimidated and isolated, e.g. John Tate isolates characters by suggesting they're on their own "side", playing them off against the rest of the group.

3) Cathy gains power using violent acts (both threatened and actual) — her willingness to hurt and even kill others means she's "running things" by the end of the play.

4) Phil uses emotional abuse to control other characters — in Act Three, he puts a "*reassuring*" hand on Lou's shoulder to manipulate her into leaving when she starts asking what's going to happen.

Power and Group Dynamics

The group has a mob mentality

1) A mob mentality is when people act the <u>same way</u> as those around them, ignoring their own feelings and principles. Their actions are based on <u>emotion</u> rather than rational thought, and can be <u>violent</u>.

2) In the play, the <u>group</u> acquires a mob mentality at times. For example, they <u>bully</u> Adam to his 'death' before the play begins — the fact that <u>principled</u> characters like Brian take part in this suggests that they are acting <u>without thought</u>.

3) Under Phil's <u>leadership</u>, the group commit increasingly <u>immoral acts</u> — they don't stop to <u>question</u> what they're doing, but go along with it because <u>everyone else</u> is.

4) In Act One, Leah's monologue about bonobos and chimps encourages the audience to make the <u>connection</u> between the actions of the <u>group</u> and the behaviour of <u>chimps</u>:

- Leah claims that humans can behave with <u>empathy</u> like bonobos or <u>violently</u> like chimps.
- She describes <u>chimps</u> hounding outsiders to the group to <u>death</u> — this is exactly what the group does to Adam.
- The similarity between the behaviour of the group and chimps occurs again when they allow Adam's <u>murder</u>. Only Leah treats Adam <u>kindly</u> and tries to <u>prevent</u> his death — her actions suggest that it is possible for humans to behave more like <u>bonobos</u>.

Physical Skills

At times when the group act violently, they could use <u>animalistic</u> body language, such as crouching on all fours, to emphasise the link to chimps.

Group dynamics change throughout the play

1) As the start of the play, the group are <u>disjointed</u> and <u>scared</u> after Adam's 'death'. The characters argue and threaten one another — John Tate says he'll "hurt" Richard, and Cathy and Danny tell each other to shut up. This suggests that the characters <u>don't get on well</u>.

2) However, in Act Two Leah reports that the group are happier now that "<u>Everyone's working together</u>" to cover up Adam's 'death' — for example, Danny and Cathy act like "old friends". Hiding the <u>secret</u> about Adam's 'death' has brought the group <u>closer together</u>.

3) Once the danger of being caught passes, the characters <u>grow apart</u> again. In Act Four, Richard hints that the characters have <u>scattered</u> — there's no suggestion that they are <u>working together</u> any more.

Social Isolation

Although they seem to have little in common, the characters spend time together <u>before</u> and <u>after</u> Adam's 'death'. This may be because of their desire to <u>belong</u> and fear of <u>social isolation</u> (see p.7).

Friendship

- Some characters within the group seem to be <u>friends</u>. Jan and Mark always appear together — their friendship seems <u>unaffected</u> by the play's events. In contrast, Leah and Phil initially always appear together, but the play's events drive them <u>apart</u>.
- <u>Proxemics</u> could be used to show these friendships. Characters who are friends could <u>stand together</u>, while those whose friendship is fading could move <u>further apart</u> as the play goes on.

© Elliott Franks/ ArenaPAL

Who needs enemies when you have friends like these...

The changing dynamics of the group affect how each character acts and how they interact with the others. Consider how a director and the performers might make these dynamics clear to the audience.

Dennis Kelly and 'DNA'

Dennis Kelly came onto the playwriting scene in the early 21st century. His plays normally examine social issues in modern society and ask difficult moral questions — just as well he's not writing the exam paper.

Dennis Kelly is a British playwright

© Heathcliff O'Malley/REX/Shutterstock

1) Dennis Kelly was born in 1970 and grew up in north London.
2) He left school at sixteen and began a series of retail jobs. During this time, he became interested in theatre and joined the Barnet Drama Centre, where he began acting and writing plays.
3) In 2000, Kelly graduated with a first class degree in Drama and Theatre Arts from the University of London. Since then, he has written many plays, including *Debris* and *Osama the Hero*. He has also written for television and film, and co-wrote the stage adaptation of *Matilda the Musical*.

His plays tend to focus on social issues

1) Kelly is known for writing plays that focus on social and political issues in modern society.
2) His plays tend to pose questions about these issues, rather than giving his views on them.
3) The issues he explores are often familiar to modern audiences, so they can easily engage with them. For example, audiences are likely to have encountered some of the issues in *DNA*, such as bullying and peer pressure.
4) Kelly's characters are usually ordinary people who have the potential to live normal lives. This makes them more relatable for the audience.
5) Kelly throws his characters into high-pressure situations where they have to make difficult moral decisions and live with the consequences. The audience is encouraged to question these decisions — in *DNA*, the audience may question whether it is ever right to sacrifice an individual for the good of the majority.
6) In many of his plays, Kelly explores social issues through shocking and violent means associated with in-yer-face theatre (see p.16). This forces audiences to face unpleasant truths in society and challenge their own moral views.

In-yer-face Theatre

Features of in-yer-face theatre, like graphic violence, appear in Kelly's other plays. In *Osama the Hero*, a student who writes a school project praising Osama bin Laden is tortured by his neighbours. This shows how fear can make people act immorally, particularly towards those who don't conform to their views.

Kelly wrote 'DNA' to be performed by youth theatre groups

1) Kelly wrote *DNA* in 2007 for the National Theatre Connections project, which commissions ten new plays each year for youth theatre groups. A professional production of *DNA* was staged a year later.
2) He wrote the play for a young cast — the characters are all teenagers in secondary school, and many of the themes are particularly relevant to young people.
3) Kelly wanted the play to be open to interpretation — in a note at the start of the play, he states that the names and genders of the characters can be changed.

EXAM TIP

"Ink!" yells Den (is my favourite anagram of 'Dennis Kelly')

Kelly explores ideas that most modern audiences will be able to relate to, but you still need to be able to say how you would perform, design or direct a production to get these ideas across to your audience.

The Play on Stage

Playwrights can be influenced by the theatre conventions of the time they live in. *DNA* was written at a time of theatrical experimentation, which helps to make it open to being performed in different ways.

British theatre was still evolving at the start of the millennium

1) <u>Before</u> the <u>1950s</u>, a lot of mainstream theatre was quite traditional. Most plays written during this time were intended to appeal to middle-class theatregoers, and plays were often staged in a <u>naturalistic</u> style (p.18).

2) From the <u>mid 20th century</u> onwards, theatre became more focused on <u>social</u> and <u>political</u> issues and featured more working-class characters. Plays written during this time were often more <u>experimental</u>.

3) <u>Non-naturalistic</u> methods (see p.18) were used more — for example <u>physical theatre</u> emerged in the late 20th century, and set designs became more <u>stylised</u> and <u>symbolic</u>.

4) By the <u>2000s</u>, a <u>wide variety</u> of different <u>styles</u> and <u>conventions</u> had been developed and were being used in British theatre. This meant that Kelly <u>didn't have</u> a clear set of conventions to follow when he wrote *DNA*.

The theatre conventions of a certain period are the features of the style of staging, design and performance that were in use at that time.

> British theatre was traditionally quite <u>conservative</u> — since the 18th century, all plays had to be <u>approved</u> before they could be performed. The <u>Theatres Act</u> of 1968 <u>ended</u> this <u>censorship</u> and playwrights began to include more <u>controversial</u> themes and content (e.g. <u>graphic violence</u>). Many of Kelly's plays include controversial elements.

Different productions of 'DNA' use different conventions

1) Directors of *DNA* have <u>experimented</u> with different theatre <u>conventions</u>.

2) Most productions of *DNA* use a <u>minimalist</u>, non-naturalistic set. For example, the first professional production of *DNA* at the National Theatre in 2008 used a <u>sparse</u> set with a black, tarmac-effect floor and minimal scenery and stage furniture.

3) Several productions have used back projections on an <u>end-on stage</u> to distinguish between the <u>three settings</u> — the National Theatre projected <u>videos</u> of a street, a field and a wood, while Hull Truck Theatre's production in 2012 projected <u>images</u> of the three locations.

© Donald Cooper/ photostage

The minimalist set of the National Theatre production allowed physical distance between the actors, highlighting the emotional distance between the characters.

4) Some productions use non-naturalistic <u>lighting design</u> to emphasise the themes of the play. The characters in the National Youth Theatre's 2016 production used <u>hand-held torches</u> at Phil's command to change which parts of the stage were lit. This highlighted Phil's power over the group.

5) Costume designers tend to choose <u>school uniforms</u> to show the characters are in secondary school, or casual clothes such as <u>hoodies</u> to locate the play in the 21st century. The actors often wear <u>coats</u> to show that the action is taking place <u>outside</u>.

6) Some productions have explored Kelly's suggestion that the names and genders of characters can be <u>changed</u> — a 2014 production at Hampton Court House school changed the male roles to female and performed the play with an <u>all-female</u> cast.

You won't need to write about adaptations in your exam, but it's useful to see how directors have presented the play in different ways — directors often use other works for inspiration.

EXAM TIP

I went to a theatre convention — everyone dressed as Hamlet...

The range of theatrical conventions in the 21st century means *DNA* can be performed in lots of ways — you just need to be able to explain the effects you're trying to create with your staging and design choices.

Practice Questions

Time for some questions — I know this is the part you've been looking forward to, so I won't keep you waiting too much longer. Start with the quick questions to see how much you've taken in from this section. Once you've finished them, have a bash at the in-depth questions — try to write about a paragraph for each one.

Quick Questions

1) Why did surveillance measures become stricter in Britain in the 21st century?

2) Briefly describe what the term 'Broken Society' means.

3) How might technology have increased social isolation amongst teenagers in the early 21st century?

4) How does Phil make sure that everyone in the group is responsible for the plan to cover up Adam's 'death'?

5) Name two characters in *DNA* who feel guilty, and briefly describe how their guilt affects them.

6) Give two examples of bullying in the play.

7) Briefly explain what a mob mentality is.

8) What type of cast was *DNA* written for?

9) True or false: theatre became less conservative in the late 20th and early 21st centuries.

In-depth Questions

1) Explain how the period in which *DNA* is set might influence your costume design for Cathy.

2) How does the characters' knowledge of DNA and its uses affect the events of the play?

3) How do the acts of bullying in the play (including the events leading to Adam's fall before the play begins) link to the theme of power?

4) Explain how public concern over the rights of individuals is reflected in the play.

5) Give two examples of theatre conventions used in past productions of the play. Would you use these conventions in a production? Give reasons for your answer.

Practice Questions

These are the type of higher mark questions you could be asked in the exam, so it's well worth taking your time and answering each one properly. Don't try to answer them all in one go — pick one, make a plan, then write a full answer. When you finish, you can imitate Phil in the one way it's sensible to do so (by grabbing a snack).

Exam-style Questions

> Read from the start of Act One ("*A Wood*") to where John Tate says "**I'm trying to keep things together**", then answer Question 1 below.

1) As a designer working on a production of the play, explain how you would use staging to portray this extract effectively to the audience. You should refer to the play's context in your answer.

> Read Act Two ("*A Field*") from the stage direction "**LEAH jumps up, shocked**" to the end of the scene, then answer Question 2 below.

2) As a designer working on a production of *DNA*, describe how you would use lighting to portray this extract effectively on stage to the audience.

> Find the part of Act Three where the group meet Adam in the wood. Read from the start of the scene to where Leah says "**Okay. Right. Okay**", then answer Question 3 below.

3) Imagine you're a director creating a production of *DNA*. Explain how a costume designer might portray this extract effectively on stage to the audience. Refer to the play's context in your answer.

> Read Act Three ("*A Wood*") from where Phil says "**Take Brian**" to the end of the scene, then answer Question 4 below.

4) Imagine you're a designer working on *DNA*. Explain how you would use props and stage furniture to portray this extract effectively on stage to the audience. You should refer to the play's context in your answer.

5) Choose one key scene from *DNA*. Explain how this scene could be designed, referring to the play's structure as well as the style, the set and the mood and atmosphere you want to create. Refer to how the first production of the play was staged in your answer.

Genre

Genre refers to what type of story a performance tells — each genre has its own style and features. *DNA* takes features from various genres and becomes its own unique beast. Don't worry, you can tame it.

'DNA' contains elements of tragedy and comedy

1) A <u>tragedy</u> is a story that is based on the <u>downfall</u> of the main character as a result of their key 'flaw'. It deals with <u>serious themes</u>, is <u>sad</u> for the audience to watch and has an <u>unhappy ending</u>.

2) In some ways, *DNA* <u>fits</u> into this genre — it contains <u>serious</u> themes and can be <u>upsetting</u> for the audience to watch. The ending is <u>unhappy</u>, as most of the characters are <u>worse off</u> than they were at the start.

3) The character of Phil includes <u>tragic elements</u> — his 'flaw' is his determination to protect the <u>group</u> at the expense of <u>individuals</u> (e.g. the postman and Adam). This leaves him <u>alone</u> and outside the group at the end of the play.

4) However, *DNA* has elements of <u>comedy</u> too — there are <u>amusing moments</u>, such as when Leah fails to predict the future, and parts that can be <u>played humorously</u>, such as Jan and Mark's duologues.

5) A director can choose to <u>emphasise</u> aspects of tragedy or comedy.

Proxemics

Phil's 'downfall' could be highlighted by having him always at the <u>centre</u> of the group with the other characters <u>crowded around him</u> in scenes in the woods, and then <u>sitting far</u> from Richard in the final scene.

Effect on the Audience

The frequent shifts from tragedy to comedy mean that tension is repeatedly <u>built</u> and <u>released</u>, which keeps the performance interesting for the audience. This also keeps the audience guessing about whether the play will end <u>happily</u> or <u>unhappily</u>.

© Helen Murray / ArenaPAL

The 'in-yer-face' aspects of the play may shock the audience

1) In-yer-face theatre emerged in <u>Britain</u> in the <u>1990s</u>. Playwrights like Sarah Kane and Mark Ravenhill wrote gritty plays containing obscene language and <u>violent</u> acts that are <u>distressing</u> to watch. In-yer-face plays often include <u>social messages</u> which may be shocking or uncomfortable for the audience to confront.

2) *DNA* includes crude language and has <u>violent</u>, in-yer-face moments, such as when Phil puts a plastic bag over Brian's head. However, <u>most</u> of the shocking events mentioned happen <u>off stage</u>, like Adam's murder.

3) The play addresses controversial <u>social issues</u>, such as gang crime and social responsibility (see p.7). Forcing the audience to consider the <u>impacts</u> of these issues on the characters in the <u>play</u> may also encourage them to think about their impact in the <u>real world</u>.

Effect on the Audience

Having <u>violent events</u> happen <u>off stage</u> means the audience isn't overwhelmed by what's happening on stage — this lets them focus on the <u>play's ideas</u> and <u>themes</u>.

REVISION TASK

Where should this revision guide be? In-yer-face...

Read Act Three ("A Street"). Write a paragraph explaining how you would direct this scene to emphasise its comic elements. Your should write about:

1) The comic aspects of this scene.
2) How actors could use vocal and physical skills to create humour.
3) The effect your choices would have on the audience.

Tick list:
✓ elements of comedy
✓ performance skills
✓ effect on audience

Structure

The structure of a play is all about how the story is put together, and what order events happen in.

The play follows a linear narrative

© Donald Cooper/photostage

1) The main plot follows the <u>group</u> as they attempt to cover up Adam's 'death' using increasingly <u>extreme</u> measures.

2) The plot advances <u>chronologically</u> (in the order that events happen). This may make it easier for the audience to immerse themselves in the play because it's more <u>realistic</u>.

3) The plot can be split into <u>four parts</u> — tension <u>builds</u> gradually in the first three parts and is <u>released</u> at the end as the situation is resolved:

- **INTRODUCTION**: The main <u>characters</u> are <u>introduced</u> and the <u>plot</u> is <u>established</u> — Phil comes up with a plan to frame a non-existent person for Adam's disappearance.
- **PROBLEM**: The situation becomes more <u>complicated</u> — an innocent man is arrested. Phil forces Brian to lie to the police and say the man is guilty.
- **CRISIS**: Something <u>goes wrong</u> for the group — Adam is alive and could reveal the truth. Phil tells Cathy and Brian to kill Adam to keep the truth hidden.
- **RESOLUTION**: The <u>crisis</u> is <u>resolved</u> — the group prevent the truth about Adam becoming known, but the characters suffer from the experience.

4) The <u>motivation</u> for the characters' actions, Adam's 'death', happens <u>before</u> the play starts. This throws the audience straight into the <u>action</u>, gripping them from the start.

5) The <u>gradual</u> revealing of information, particularly in Jan and Mark's duologues (see p.39), keeps up the <u>pace</u> of the play. This maintains the audience's <u>interest</u> as they work out what's going on.

The structure repeats itself

1) There are <u>fourteen</u> short scenes in *DNA*. In the first three acts, the same four scenes <u>repeat</u> in a <u>pattern</u>:

A STREET — <u>Jan</u> and <u>Mark</u> discuss what's happening.	**A FIELD** — <u>Leah</u> talks to <u>Phil</u>, who ignores her.	**A WOOD** — the <u>group</u> plan their next move.	**A FIELD** — <u>Leah</u> talks to <u>Phil</u>. The topics of her monologues <u>build suspense</u> for the next act.

Staging and Design

A designer needs to consider how to design the set to make the three settings <u>distinctive</u>.

2) The scenes in each act give <u>different characters'</u> views on events — this gives the audience a variety of <u>perspectives</u> on what's happening.

3) The <u>cyclical</u> repetition of the settings creates <u>tension</u> for the audience. It hints that the characters are <u>trapped</u> in a loop, unable to escape from their situation, which gradually gets worse and worse.

4) The last act <u>breaks</u> this cycle by only having two scenes. This could leave the audience with a sense that the issues raised are <u>unresolved</u>.

Set Design

The <u>stage</u> could become <u>messier</u> as the play goes on, for example with empty carrier bags and discarded shopping trolleys, to <u>emphasise</u> the increasingly chaotic situation the group is in.

EXAM TIP

This play is like a washing machine — it goes in cycles...

You should think about the effects of the play's structure and how your design or performance choices could build on these effects. You never know your luck — it just might come in handy on exam day...

Style

Style is all about how a play is produced — the style is chosen by the director. Decisions, decisions...

'DNA' includes naturalistic elements...

For more on how different styles are staged, see Section Four.

1) <u>Naturalism</u> is a style of theatre that aims to recreate <u>real life</u> on stage. The audience should <u>forget</u> that they're in a <u>theatre</u> and be able to <u>imagine</u> that what they're watching is <u>real</u>.

2) The characters in *DNA* speak in a <u>realistic</u> way for modern teenagers (see p.22). This makes the performance seem more <u>authentic</u> and allows the audience to feel as though they are present in the story.

3) The events of the play follow a <u>linear</u> order, which makes it easier for the audience to <u>suspend their disbelief</u>.

4) None of the characters acknowledge they are in a play or <u>break</u> the '<u>fourth wall</u>' (see p.43). They only communicate with each other, which means the audience is <u>not</u> brought out of the story.

Effect on the Audience

Most audiences will come into contact with this style of <u>language</u> on a day-to-day basis, making it easier for them to <u>relate</u> to the play's characters.

5) Directors and designers can <u>emphasise</u> naturalistic features of the play using:

- <u>Lighting design</u> — a designer could use lighting that would create a realistic impression of the three <u>settings</u>, such as using a spotlight with an orange gel to suggest <u>streetlights</u> for scenes set in a street.
- <u>Costume design</u> — costumes that reflect what many 21st century <u>teenagers wear</u>, such as school uniforms and hoodies, could be used to make the characters seem more authentic.
- <u>Sound design</u> — a designer could use sound effects that would be heard in each of the three <u>settings</u>, such as <u>birdsong</u> in the wood or <u>cars</u> passing in the street.

... but a director could use a non-naturalistic style

1) <u>Non-naturalistic</u> theatre includes features that remind an audience that what they're watching <u>isn't real</u>. This encourages them to <u>focus</u> on the play's <u>themes</u> and the <u>questions</u> it raises.

2) Kelly's stage directions are <u>short</u>, e.g. "*A Field*", so a director can <u>interpret</u> them however they want. The play could be staged with a <u>minimalist</u> set (see p.45) to make the settings more <u>symbolic</u> than realistic.

Set Design

It's hard to stage three <u>realistic outdoor</u> settings in a theatre, so a non-naturalistic set is more <u>practical</u>.

© Helen Murray / ArenaPAL

3) <u>Lighting</u> could also be used in a non-naturalistic way. For example, a <u>spotlight</u> could be focused on Phil when he explains his plan to the group to <u>highlight</u> the group's attention.

4) <u>Physical</u> theatre techniques, such as dance or mime, could be used to re-enact events that happen <u>off-stage</u> while the characters talk about them. For example, <u>Phil's plan</u> could be acted out as he tells each character what to do.

REVISION TASK

It's only natural that you want to keep revising...

Choose a scene and decide whether you would produce it in a naturalistic or non-naturalistic style. Write a paragraph about either set design, lighting, sound or costume. You should consider:

1) The aspects of the style you want to use.
2) How you would emphasise your chosen style.
3) The effect of this style on the audience.

Tick list:
✓ one style type
✓ specific examples of how to create style
✓ effect on audience

Stage Directions

Stage directions tell performers how they should do things. They also communicate changes in setting, who is on stage, and entrances and exits. They're pretty darn important, but Kelly only uses them when he needs to.

Stage directions in 'DNA' are limited

1) *DNA* has <u>fewer</u> stage directions than most plays, and the stage directions Kelly includes are often <u>short</u> and not very detailed. This means the play is open to <u>interpretation</u> and can be produced in many ways.

2) Longer stage directions are normally spaced out over <u>several lines</u>. This suggests how actors could perform these actions. For example:

- When Leah attempts to <u>strangle</u> herself in Act One, the structure of the stage directions suggests the performer should make the action last for a <u>long time</u>. This creates <u>suspense</u> for the audience. It also highlights Phil's <u>lack of empathy</u> — he has many chances to <u>intervene</u> but chooses not to.
- As the group waits for Phil to come up with a plan in Act One, there is "*Silence*" followed by "*More silence*" on the next line, emphasising the <u>length</u> of the pause. On the next line, Phil puts down his drink — an actor could make this a slow, <u>deliberate</u> act to draw the <u>audience's attention</u> to him.

Physical contact shows when characters are being controlling

Stage directions can show how characters assert their <u>authority</u> through <u>physical contact</u>. For example:

- In Act One, John Tate <u>silences</u> Leah by placing "*a finger on her lips*". This action could be performed in an <u>intimidating</u> way to show that John is using physical contact to maintain <u>control</u> of the group.
- In Act Three, Phil <u>stops</u> Lou from asking <u>questions</u> about what's going to happen to Adam — he "*Places a hand on her shoulder, smiles, warm, reassuring.*" The action isn't reassuring, but the stage direction suggests how Phil wants it to <u>appear</u> to Lou.

© Elliott Franks/ ArenaPAL

Pauses can have different effects

1) Kelly uses a lot of <u>pauses</u> and <u>beats</u> (brief pauses that change the rhythm or course of a scene).

2) They can indicate a <u>moment of realisation</u> — in Act Three, Leah's insight that Phil doesn't intend to help Adam is shown by a <u>beat</u>. In this moment, an actor playing Leah could use <u>physical skills</u>, such as widening her eyes, to show her realisation.

3) Pauses can be used to <u>build tension</u> — in Act Two, Phil pauses <u>before</u> threatening to throw Brian down the mineshaft. This focuses the audience's <u>attention</u> on Phil's threat, which gives it more weight.

4) They can also indicate a change of <u>direction</u> in a character's <u>thoughts</u> — at the end of Act One, Leah pauses after her monologue about bonobos before she says "We're in trouble now". This pause indicates a shift in <u>mood</u> from cheerful to tense — an actor could frown or bite her lip to highlight this shift.

REVISION TASK

I don't like bears — their big paws make me tense...

Choose a short section of the play with at least two pauses or beats. Write a paragraph about how you would direct this section of the play. Make sure you cover:

1) What effect you want the pauses to have on the audience.
2) The vocal skills you would tell actors to use before and after the pauses.
3) Any physical skills you would direct actors to use.

Tick list:
✓ effect on the audience
✓ vocal skills
✓ physical skills

Settings

Although the settings are important, Kelly doesn't give much information about them in his stage directions. That's where this page comes in — it tells you everything you need to know.

'DNA' is set in a generic town

1) There are <u>three settings</u> in the play — a street, a field and a wood.

2) The three settings are <u>generic</u> locations that will feel <u>familiar</u> to the audience. This makes the play's events feel like they could happen <u>anywhere</u>, which makes them more <u>unsettling</u> for the audience.

3) Some of the play's <u>events</u> also occur <u>off stage</u> in other locations around the town:

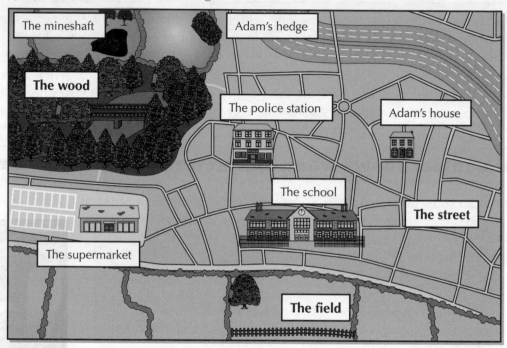

The mineshaft | Adam's hedge

The wood

The police station | Adam's house

The school

Adam's house

The street

The supermarket

The field

The three settings are symbolic

You should consider what each setting <u>symbolises</u> when you design a set:

For ideas on how to design these locations on stage, see Section Four.

The Wood
- The wood is <u>isolated</u> from society, and the events that occur there are <u>hidden</u> from view. As it's the place where all the group's plans to cover up Adam's 'death' come about, it symbolises <u>secrecy</u>.
- Forest is also the natural habitat of the <u>bonobos</u> and <u>chimps</u> from Leah's monologue in Act One. This prompts the audience to compare the <u>group's behaviour</u> to that of these animals.

The Field
- The field is <u>open</u> compared to the wood. Leah and Phil seem most able to be <u>themselves</u> here, so the field could symbolise their <u>escape</u> from the pressures of the group.
- It could be a <u>romantic</u> spot, but Phil refuses to <u>communicate</u> with Leah. This could affect design choices.

The Street
- The street is likely to be the most <u>familiar</u> setting for <u>audiences</u>, making it seem <u>ordinary</u>.
- As the setting that is closest to <u>civilisation</u>, a designer could reference society, e.g. by using road signs or street lamps. This would remind the audience that the play has a wider <u>social setting</u>.

Adam's dead — I heard it on the street...

The minimal descriptions that Kelly uses for his settings means you have freedom to decide how to stage these locations. You'll need to be able to explain your choices and what effect your staging creates.

Mood and Atmosphere

Knowing how a director can create mood and atmosphere may relieve some of your exam-related tension.

The three settings have different atmospheres

© Helen Murray / ArenaPAL

1) The wood has a <u>claustrophobic</u> atmosphere because almost everyone is on stage. When the characters are together, the <u>clashes</u> between them creates <u>tension</u> — the audience doesn't know whether the group will turn on each other.

2) The street has a <u>tense</u>, <u>uncertain</u> atmosphere. This is created by Jan and Mark's rapid, fragmented duologues, which leave the audience <u>guessing</u> what's going on.

3) The field has a <u>calmer</u> atmosphere because there is often only <u>one character</u> speaking. The monologues allow for <u>reflection</u> on the play's themes and events.

4) As the play goes on, the atmosphere in each setting becomes <u>more intense</u>. The mood in the wood becomes more <u>fearful</u> as the characters grow more violent, the street scenes create more <u>uncertainty</u> as vital information is withheld, and the field becomes a place of <u>sadness</u> after Leah leaves.

Sound can help create particular moods

Kelly doesn't specify any <u>sound</u> effects that should be used, but there are references to sounds in the stage directions that can add to <u>mood</u>:

For more on sound, see p.50-51.

- Brian enters in Act One "*crying*" and doesn't stop until John Tate speaks to him. Brian's persistent crying adds to the <u>troubling mood</u>, as it hints to the audience that the group's situation is <u>really bad</u>.
- Brian's "*giggling*" when Adam returns in Act Three creates a <u>disturbing mood</u>. The laughter is a <u>jarring contrast</u> to the serious situation the group are in, which could add to the audience's <u>discomfort</u>.
- The final scene of Act Three opens with "*Complete silence*" before Leah "*begins to quietly cry*". Her silence and quiet crying <u>contrasts</u> with her previous chattiness and creates a <u>sorrowful mood</u>.

Think about when and how the atmosphere changes

Knowing when and how the atmosphere <u>changes</u> can help you make <u>design</u> or <u>performance choices</u> that support the action of the play. For example:

- In Act One ("*A Wood*"), John Tate's <u>threatening</u> "*walk towards*" Brian creates a <u>tense</u> atmosphere. This tension is <u>broken</u> by Leah and Phil's entrance — as Phil is the more dominant character, his presence causes John Tate to <u>back down</u>, while Leah's rambling speech adds a note of <u>comedy</u>.
- In the first "*Field*" scene in Act Two, there is a <u>charged</u> atmosphere when Leah mentions Adam's parents' TV appeal, and it seems as though Phil might respond. <u>Jan and Mark's arrival</u>, and Jan's statement "We need to talk", creates an <u>ominous</u> atmosphere as the audience wonder what has happened.
- Leah's <u>desperation</u> and <u>repeated pleas</u> to Phil create a <u>frantic</u> atmosphere at the end of Act Three ("*A Wood*"). This shifts to a <u>sorrowful</u> atmosphere in the following scene as Phil and Leah sit in "*silence*".

Teepee, wigwam, teepee, wigwam — I'm two tents...

Before the exam, it's a good idea to think about what mood you'd want to create at key points in the play. Then decide how you might use different elements of design and performance to create each mood.

Speech and Language

Whether you like to natter on like Leah or speak once in a blue moon like Phil, how a character talks can sometimes tell the audience more than what they actually say. It'll all make sense after these two pages.

Kelly uses colloquial language to create realistic dialogue

Kelly uses <u>naturalistic</u> dialogue — characters talk like real people do, which makes the play more lifelike. Kelly also uses language that is <u>realistic</u> for <u>21st-century teenagers</u>:

1) The characters use <u>everyday</u> phrases (e.g. "This is a nightmare") and <u>slang</u> (e.g. "proper dead").

2) Some characters use <u>crude</u> language to emphasise their panic — for example Lou repeatedly says the group are "screwed."

3) Dialogue includes <u>hesitations</u> and <u>repetition</u>, e.g. "I'm, I'm, this is it."

4) Characters frequently <u>interrupt</u> one another, just as people do in <u>real life</u>.

Physical Skills

Some <u>slang terms</u> may confuse the audience. Actors could use <u>gestures</u> to make their meaning clear — for example, Mark could pretend to <u>throw</u> a stone when he says that someone "pegged a stone" at Adam.

Vocal Skills

Actors need to <u>time</u> their interruptions well — it should sound like one character is <u>cutting another off</u>, but the audience still needs to <u>hear</u> everything that <u>both</u> characters say.

Speech shows a character's status in the group

Different <u>language styles</u> help show a character's <u>position</u> in the group hierarchy:

- <u>Stronger</u> characters often <u>tell</u> other characters what to do — Phil uses a series of <u>commands</u> to tell the group how to cover up Adam's 'death'.

- <u>Weaker characters</u> tend to use single words or <u>short phrases</u>. They are often <u>spoken over</u> or forced to <u>stop</u> talking — for example, Phil talks over Brian when he forces him to go to the police station.

- Weaker characters, including Lou and Jan, tend to ask stronger characters <u>questions</u>. John Tate uses questions differently — he <u>challenges</u> other characters in order to <u>isolate</u> them and <u>force</u> them to agree with him.

- However, John Tate's use of <u>pauses</u>, <u>fillers</u> and <u>repetition</u> (e.g. "we're not... it's not...we're not...") suggests that he is <u>insecure</u> in his role as <u>leader</u>.

An actor playing John Tate could use questioning body language, such as open palms, as he challenges other characters.

Language can create humour

Comic moments can <u>lighten</u> the mood:

1) <u>Crude language</u> can be used to relieve tension — Jan's use of the expletive "Shit" in Act Two ("*A Street*") could be funny if the actor pauses beforehand and <u>emphasises</u> the word.

2) The <u>uncertainty</u> with which characters speak can add humour. In Act One, John Tate <u>interrupts</u> himself to express his concerns about Lou's fear of Richard — this could be <u>exaggerated</u> to highlight his <u>false bravado</u>.

3) In Act Three, Brian's excited <u>exclamations</u> of "This is great! Mates!" may make the audience laugh because his tone is so <u>inappropriate</u> to the seriousness of the situation. However, the audience are also likely to feel <u>uneasy</u> at their reaction, as Brian is clearly mentally ill.

Effect on the Audience

The <u>laughter</u> from the audience would further <u>undermine</u> John Tate's weak authority, making the audience feel a <u>part</u> of the play.

Speech and Language

Monologues help to develop characters and relationships...

1) A <u>monologue</u> is when a character makes a <u>speech</u> to <u>another character</u> or to the <u>audience</u>.

2) The <u>language</u> in Leah's monologues reveals aspects of her character:

> • Leah doesn't always finish her sentences, and her monologues are full of <u>hesitations</u>, <u>fillers</u> and <u>repetition</u>. This shows her <u>low self-esteem</u> and <u>uncertainty</u> about what she's saying.
>
> • Leah asks Phil questions in her monologues but then <u>answers</u> them herself, possibly out of fear of his expected silence. This suggests that she feels <u>unsure</u> where she stands with Phil, but that she is also desperate for his <u>attention</u>.

3) Phil's speech near the end of Act One can be viewed as a monologue — other characters <u>speak</u> but he largely <u>ignores</u> them. His lack of <u>two-way</u> communication makes him seem single-minded and sets him apart from the rest of the group. Phil uses <u>full sentences</u> and <u>doesn't hesitate</u> during his monologue — this shows his ability to think <u>clearly</u> and <u>coherently</u>, even under pressure, and highlights his <u>self-confidence</u>.

An actor playing Leah could repeatedly try to engage Phil during her monologues, for example by attempting to make eye contact.

4) Adam's monologue in Act Three includes lots of pauses, fillers and repetition. He struggles to form coherent <u>sentences</u> — this reflects his disturbed <u>mental state</u>.

Performance Skills

Understanding characters' <u>feelings</u> could help an actor <u>perform</u> their monologues naturally.

... and duologues can build tension

1) A <u>duologue</u> is when <u>two characters</u> have a <u>conversation</u> together.

2) Jan and Mark have a duologue at the <u>start</u> of each act. They use questions and vague responses that only give <u>snippets</u> of information to the audience. This <u>hooks</u> the audience as they want to know what's happening.

Performance Skills

These scenes could be played <u>comically</u>, with Mark getting <u>frustrated</u> with Jan as she continues to <u>not understand</u> what's going on.

3) Jan and Mark have another duologue in Act One ("*A Wood*") when they tell the group how Adam 'died'. This duologue is full of short, <u>overlapping sentences</u> — these <u>slow</u> the story down and create <u>suspense</u> as Jan and Mark chime in with clarifications to one another's version of events.

4) This duologue is also full of <u>contradictions</u>, e.g. Mark says that Adam was "laughing" right before Jan says "and crying". This creates <u>uncertainty</u> for the audience as they wait to <u>learn</u> what happened to Adam.

Directing 'DNA'

The rest of the group, including Adam, could <u>act out</u> the events of Adam's 'death' as Jan and Mark speak — witnessing such a brutal act of bullying would add to the <u>audience's unease</u>.

EXAM TIP

A lonely tree talking to itself — a monologue...

In the exam, you might need to write about how a performer could interpret certain lines. You'll need to explain your choices too — make sure you can justify why you'd have a character speak in a certain way.

Section Two — Playwright's Techniques

Practice Questions

There's a lot to get your head around in this section, so have a go at these questions to see how much you've taken on board. If there are any questions that you're not sure about, read back over the section.

Quick Questions

1) Give one feature of in-yer-face theatre that is used in the play.

2) Which event is the crisis of the play?

3) Briefly describe one effect of the cyclical repetition of the settings in the play.

4) Give two naturalistic elements of the play.

5) Give an example of how one character uses physical contact to control another character.

6) What does the setting of *"A Wood"* symbolise?

7) How do Jan and Mark's duologues affect the atmosphere of the scenes set in *"A Street"*?

8) Give two ways in which Kelly makes the characters' dialogue realistic.

9) How does John Tate use questions to gain power over other characters?

10) What does Phil's monologue in Act One (*"A Wood"*) show about his character?

In-depth Questions

1) Explain how you would design the set for *DNA* to create a claustrophobic atmosphere for the scenes set in *"A Wood"*.

2) When Adam appears in Act Three, the stage directions say that he *"looks as though he might run off at any moment."* How might an actor use physical skills to communicate this to the audience?

3) Imagine you are directing a production of *DNA*. Would you emphasise or downplay the comedic elements of the play? Give reasons for your answer.

4) Describe how Kelly builds tension in Act One (*"A Wood"*), and explain how this affects the mood of the play.

Practice Questions

Now have a bash at these exam-style questions. For the full exam experience, you could shut yourself in a silent room and get a friend to pace around behind you, shouting "Half an hour left". Or you could, you know... not.

Exam-style Questions

> Read Act One ("*A Wood*") from where John Tate says "**What do we do?**" to the end of the act, then answer Questions 1 and 2 below.

1) Imagine you are a lighting designer for a production of *DNA*. Explain how you would use lighting to portray this extract effectively on stage for the audience.

2) Imagine you are directing a production of *DNA*. Explain how a performer playing the role of Phil might demonstrate his high status in the group to the audience in this extract and throughout the play. You should consider physical skills, vocal skills and the use of stage space in your answer.

> Read Act Two ("*A Wood*") from the start of the scene to where Danny says "**How am I gonna get references?**", then answer Question 3 below.

3) Explain how a performer playing the role of Danny could portray his character to the audience in this extract. You should consider vocal skills, physical skills and interactions with other characters.

> Read Act Three ("*A Street*"), then answer Questions 4 and 5 below.

4) Imagine you are playing Jan in this extract. Suggest **three** ways in which you would use performance skills to portray Jan's uncertainty to the audience in this extract. Give a reason for each of your suggestions.

5) Imagine you are directing a production of *DNA*. Discuss how you would use **either** staging **or** set design **or** props and stage furniture to portray this extract effectively to the audience. You should refer to the context of the play in your answer.

Character Performance — Leah

You're probably familiar with the plot by now, so it's about time you got to know the characters. This section takes you through them one by one and offers lots of suggestions on how they might be performed on stage.

Leah is a sympathetic character

1) Kelly doesn't provide any <u>background information</u> about Leah, so it's up to the actor to figure out what <u>motivates</u> her. This will have a significant impact on the way that she's performed.

2) Initially, Leah appears to be <u>devoted</u> to Phil — she remains <u>loyal</u> to him even though he largely ignores her, and she <u>supports</u> him when he becomes the new leader of the group.

© Arno Declair

> **Leah is...**
>
> **talkative**: "I talk too much, so shoot me."
> **frustrated**: "You don't care, do you."
> **principled**: "We can't just leave him up here."

Kelly doesn't give much information about Leah and Phil's history. A director might decide to interpret them as a couple or just as friends.

3) Leah <u>isn't</u> directly involved in <u>bullying</u> Adam, but she <u>is</u> caught up in the <u>aftermath</u>. Her monologues hint that she is <u>uncomfortable</u> with the group's decision to cover up Adam's 'death' and knows it is <u>morally wrong</u>. She <u>doesn't act</u> on her feelings because the plan was <u>Phil's idea</u> and she wants his <u>approval</u>.

4) Leah realises that the cover-up has gone <u>too far</u> when the postman is arrested. She begins expressing her <u>disapproval</u> to the group, which implies that she's becoming <u>frustrated</u> with their immoral behaviour.

5) After Adam is killed, Leah <u>rejects</u> the rest of the group completely. She "*Storms*" away from Phil, then the audience finds out that she has "*Moved schools*". This suggests that Leah has finally decided to put her <u>principles</u> before her <u>loyalty</u> to Phil.

> **Effect on the Audience**
>
> Leah's <u>conflicting emotions</u> make her <u>more relatable</u> than the rest of the group. She considers the <u>moral consequences</u> of her actions, which makes it easier for the audience to understand her.

She seeks Phil's approval for most of the play

1) The scenes that take place in "*A Field*" make Leah and Phil's relationship seem <u>one-sided</u>. Leah <u>admires</u> Phil and tries to engage him in conversation, but he <u>rarely responds</u>, no matter what she does.

2) The way that Leah talks to Phil suggests that she has <u>low self-esteem</u>. This is particularly obvious in her <u>opening monologue</u> in Act One — she's convinced that Phil is thinking "<u>negative</u>" thoughts about her.

3) An actor playing Leah needs to communicate Leah's desire for Phil's <u>attention</u> and her lack of <u>self-esteem</u> to the audience:

> **Physical Skills**
>
> • Leah could stay in <u>close proximity</u> to Phil in their scenes together to stress her <u>admiration</u> for him.
>
> • An actor playing Leah might repeatedly try to <u>establish eye contact</u> with Phil while she speaks. This would suggest that Leah wants to see whether or not Phil <u>reacts</u> to what she's saying.
>
> • An actor could also use <u>exaggerated movements</u> and <u>gestures</u> in an attempt to gain Phil's <u>attention</u> — for example, she might <u>brandish</u> the Tupperware® container in his face during Act Two.
>
> • It's <u>disheartening</u> for Leah when Phil doesn't respond, so an actor might use a <u>slouched posture</u> and a <u>disappointed facial expression</u> to convey this. This might attract <u>sympathy</u> from the audience.

Character Performance — Leah

Leah is forced to talk to herself

1) Phil's silence causes Leah to keep talking. This means that scenes with these two characters are like a stream of consciousness for Leah, in which she says the first thing that comes to mind.

2) An actor playing Leah needs to think carefully about vocal performance for her monologues:

© Hull Truck Theatre

Vocal Skills

- Leah comes across as lively and animated when she talks to Phil. An actor might speak loudly and at a fast pace to add to the impression that she's trying to get his attention.

- However, Leah's emotions change regularly throughout each speech — she often lapses into moments of thoughtfulness or melancholy. An actor should use varying stress and intonation to communicate this wide range of emotions to the audience.

- Leah uses filler words like "you know" or "I mean", as if she's only speaking to fill the silence. An actor could use frequent pauses to show that Leah's trying to think of what to say next.

She lacks authority in group scenes

1) Leah has little power in the scenes that take place in "A Wood". She isn't an authority figure like Phil or John Tate, so she finds it difficult to communicate her point of view to the rest of the group.

2) In the "Wood" scenes, an actor might reflect Leah's lack of power using physical and vocal skills:

Physical Skills

- An actor could stand towards the edge of the stage to emphasise Leah's minimal authority in the group.

- She disagrees with many of the group's decisions, so an actor may use reserved body language. This would suggest that Leah doesn't want to be involved in the plan, but lacks the authority to challenge it.

Vocal Skills

- In Act One, an actor could stumble over her words when Leah tells John Tate that she and Phil "haven't done anything" to give the sense that Leah is nervous about standing up to John Tate.

- When Leah speaks in Act Two, there's still a sense that she's unsure of herself. An actor could use a doubtful tone to express Leah's concern about lying to the authorities ("Maybe we could do nothing?").

- Leah is often interrupted by the others, particularly in Act Three ("A Wood"). An actor could speak hesitantly at the start of this scene to highlight that she has less authority than some other characters.

She becomes increasingly frustrated

1) In Act Three ("A Wood"), Leah starts to lose patience with Phil and the other characters. She's the only one to suggest helping Adam and she objects when the rest of the group agree to maintain the cover-up.

2) Leah is concerned about Adam's welfare, so an actor might speak to him in a soft and caring voice. This would show that Leah is aware of Adam's fragile condition (see p.34-35) and wants to help him.

3) However, an actor might raise her voice when she speaks to Phil — "No! Stop, don't, don't, Phil". This would suggest that she's shocked and angry when she realises that Phil plans to have Adam killed.

4) An actor's body language might become more tense and agitated as the scene progresses — she could clench her fists tightly or grit her teeth to express her increasing anxiety and frustration to the audience.

Section Three — Character and Performance

Character Performance — Leah

Leah cracks towards the end of the play

1) Act Three finishes with another short scene between Leah and Phil. Leah was <u>unable</u> to stop Adam's murder in the previous scene, but her behaviour towards Phil makes her <u>disapproval</u> clear.

2) Leah <u>doesn't speak</u> at all in this scene. This <u>contrasts</u> with earlier scenes and presents an actor with a new challenge — she needs to show Leah's <u>anger</u> towards Phil using her <u>physical</u> performance:

© Michael Smith/ Auckland Theatre Company

In this production, Leah (changed to Lee and played by a male actor) faces away from Phil.

Physical Skills

- At the start of this scene, an actor might sit with <u>her arms folded</u> and <u>her back slightly turned</u> to Phil. This would suggest that Leah is <u>disgusted</u> with Phil for his decision to have Adam murdered.

- An actor playing Leah may <u>flinch</u> when Phil puts his arm around her, as though she can't even stand to be touched by him anymore.

- Leah's rejection of Phil is an <u>important moment</u>, so an actor should draw the audience's attention to it. She might spit the sweet out in an <u>exaggerated</u> manner, before <u>pushing Phil away</u> from her <u>roughly</u>. This would emphasise how <u>strongly</u> she is rejecting Phil.

- The stage directions say that Leah "<u>*Storms off*</u>", so an actor might use <u>quick</u>, <u>heavy footsteps</u>. She may exit the stage <u>without looking back</u> to make Leah's rejection of Phil seem <u>decisive</u> to the audience.

Use specific details when you're writing about performance

Take a look at the sample answer <u>below</u>. It shows how you could write about performing Leah <u>in the exam</u>:

> When Leah first appears on stage in Act One, she seems needy and insecure. An actor could fidget nervously by picking their fingers or biting their nails when asking Phil "What are you thinking?" to suggest that Leah is anxious to know Phil's response. When Phil doesn't respond, she might wave her hand casually and say "Not that I'm bothered" in a dismissive tone of voice to show Leah is pretending not to care. However, a worried expression would reveal to the audience that she's still preoccupied with Phil's thoughts about her.

This makes a <u>clear point</u> about Leah's character.

This clearly focuses on a <u>specific moment</u>.

This explains the <u>intended effect</u> on the <u>audience</u>.

REVISION TASK

I'd have left when he didn't offer me any of that waffle...

Read Act Three ("A Field") from "LEAH turns up. She is carrying a suitcase" to "LEAH sags." Write two paragraphs on how you would perform the role of Leah here. You should consider:

1) Your vocal delivery (e.g. volume, pace, pitch).
2) Your body language and use of space on stage.
3) The effect of these decisions on the audience.

Tick list:
- ✓ vocal performance
- ✓ physical performance
- ✓ effect on the audience

Section Three — Character and Performance

Character Performance — Phil

You'd be forgiven for thinking that it's easy to play someone who barely says a word, but you'd be wrong. Phil's a complicated character and the role requires an actor to make the most of their performance skills.

Phil becomes the group's leader

1) Phil is rarely seen on stage without Leah, but he is often <u>silent</u> and almost <u>never</u> acknowledges her.
2) He isn't involved in Adam's 'death', but John Tate asks him to come up with a plan because he's "<u>clever</u>". The group don't object to this <u>change in leadership</u>, which suggests that they <u>look up to Phil</u>.

> **Phil is...**
>
> **uncommunicative:** *"PHIL says nothing."*
> **threatening:** *"If you don't help us we'll kill you."*
> **authoritative:** *"Tell no one or we'll all go to prison."*

© ROBERT WORKMAN/ArenaPAL

3) As the leader of the group, Phil goes to <u>extreme lengths</u> to ensure that the cover-up remains intact — he doesn't hesitate to threaten the rest of the group, and he instructs Cathy to <u>kill</u> Adam when it turns out that he's <u>alive</u> after all.

His intentions aren't clear

1) Phil's reasons for coming up with a plan to cover up Adam's 'death' aren't clear, but it's possible that he's trying to <u>protect</u> the group. In Act Three ("*A Wood*"), when Leah challenges his decision to return Adam to the hedge, Phil asks "What's more important; <u>one person</u> or <u>everyone</u>?" He believes that <u>sacrificing</u> one person is <u>justified</u> if it benefits everyone else.
2) However, it's also possible that Phil is an <u>immoral character</u> who <u>enjoys</u> the challenge of misleading the police — he might be putting the rest of the group at risk for his own <u>entertainment</u>.
3) Phil doesn't take an <u>active role</u> in the cover-up. In Act One ("*A Wood*"), he gives <u>everyone</u> in the group a task to perform apart from Leah and himself. This might be because Phil and Leah weren't involved in Adam's 'death', but it might also suggest that Phil wants to avoid the <u>blame</u> if the cover-up goes <u>wrong</u>.

His physical presence is important

1) Phil's <u>appearance</u> isn't described in the stage directions. However, it's important that his physical presence on stage supports his <u>characterisation</u>:

Physical Skills

- Phil is a teenager like the rest of the group, but he comes across as <u>more mature</u>. An actor might use <u>slow</u>, <u>decisive movements</u> to show that Phil is more <u>controlled</u> and less <u>nervous</u> than the other characters.
- To achieve a similar effect, an actor could <u>remain still</u> throughout the play — this could contrast with the others twitching and fidgeting.
- An actor may also use an <u>upright posture</u> to make Phil seem <u>taller</u> and more <u>self-assured</u> than the others. This would emphasise his <u>authority</u>.

Stage Position

An actor's <u>stage position</u> can affect how a character appears to the audience. An actor playing Phil might stick to a <u>centre stage position</u> in order to stress his <u>importance</u>.

2) It's important to consider the impact of Phil's physicality on the rest of the group. If he's portrayed as a <u>physically imposing</u> character, it will make sense to the audience if the others react with <u>fear</u> or <u>respect</u>.

Section Three — Character and Performance

Character Performance — Phil

Phil is largely unresponsive to Leah

1) Phil plays a <u>passive role</u> during the scenes that take place in "*A Field*". There are signs that he's <u>listening</u> to Leah, but he <u>barely reacts</u> to her — he usually focuses on whatever he's eating or drinking at the time.

2) Although Phil doesn't do or say much in these scenes, an actor's use of <u>physical skills</u> remains <u>important</u>:

- An actor playing Phil could <u>remain still</u> to suggest a <u>lack of interest</u> in what Leah is saying. He occasionally moves to eat or drink something — an actor might do this <u>slowly</u> and <u>intently</u>.
- An actor might also put on a <u>neutral facial expression</u> and <u>stare into the distance</u> while Leah is talking. This would make it hard for the audience to <u>judge his reaction</u> to what she's saying.
- However, an actor could give the audience <u>subtle clues</u> about Phil's <u>thoughts</u>. For example, he might <u>raise an eyebrow</u> to show <u>surprise</u> when Leah says that Brian has started taking medication.

Effect on the Audience

Phil's silence in the "*Field*" scenes could be played in different ways to have different effects on the audience. For example, if an actor focuses <u>obsessively</u> on his food and seems <u>oblivious</u> to Leah, his silence may seem <u>comical</u>. At other moments, an actor could <u>frown</u> or <u>clench his jaw</u> to make it seem as though he is <u>irritated</u> — this could create an <u>ominous</u> mood for the audience.

He's calm and collected under pressure

1) In the scenes that take place in "*A Wood*", Phil's behaviour changes completely — he's a <u>commanding</u> figure who <u>dominates</u> the action.

2) This change in Phil's behaviour requires an actor to use <u>physical skills</u> differently in these scenes compared to the "*Field*" scenes:

This actor uses an unconcerned facial expression to show that Phil is calm and in control.

© Hull Truck Theatre

Physical Skills

- In Act One, an actor playing Phil might move into a <u>centre stage position</u> when John Tate asks him what to do about Adam — this would imply that Phil is <u>taking control</u> as the group's <u>new leader</u>.
- Phil could become more animated. In Act Two, an actor might use <u>controlled</u> but <u>expressive gestures</u>, such as pointing at each member of the group in turn, when he tells them to keep their "mouths shut".
- In Act Three, an actor could emphasise Phil's <u>dominance</u> over the other characters using <u>physical contact</u>. He might approach Jan and Mark and place his arms around their shoulders before <u>ordering</u> them to return home and tell no one about Adam.

3) Another way that Phil's behaviour changes with the group is that he starts to <u>speak</u>, but only when it's <u>completely necessary</u>. Unlike the rest of the group, he doesn't just speak his mind without thinking.

Vocal Skills

- An actor could use a <u>calm</u>, <u>measured tone</u> to match Phil's <u>relaxed appearance</u>. This would also provide a contrast to the anxiety of the other characters, who often <u>talk excitedly</u> over each other.
- He could also use <u>clear diction</u> and <u>regular phrasing</u>. This would make Phil sound <u>authoritative</u>.
- An actor's vocal delivery might become <u>menacing</u> when other characters <u>refuse</u> to follow orders. For example, he may speak to Brian in a <u>low-pitched growl</u> when Brian refuses to go to the police station — "You have to go in." This would suggest that Phil is struggling to control his <u>temper</u>.

Character Performance — Phil

Phil can be brutal and callous...

1) There are signs that Phil is a <u>violent</u> individual throughout the play. For example, he convinces Brian to lie to the police by threatening to throw him into the same hole as Adam so that they can "<u>rot together</u>".

2) This side to Phil's character is <u>more obvious</u> in Act Three. Although he doesn't <u>commit violence</u> himself, he shows Cathy and Brian how to suffocate Adam with a plastic bag, before sending them away to do it.

3) To heighten the impact of these moments on the audience, an actor might suggest that Phil is <u>unaffected</u> by his behaviour. This could be achieved by speaking in a <u>low pitched</u>, <u>quiet voice</u> with <u>minimal intonation</u> or using a <u>blank expression</u> whenever violence is mentioned ("I'm gonna do an experiment with this plastic bag.").

© Arno Declair

Effect on the Audience

There's a good chance that the audience will see Phil as a <u>psychopath</u> if an actor highlights the merciless side of his character. His actions might seem <u>more shocking</u> if the audience are led to believe that he feels <u>no remorse</u> for Adam's <u>murder</u>.

A psychopath can behave anti-socially, immorally or even violently without feeling remorse.

... but he shows signs of a softer side in the end

1) Phil's behaviour at the end of the play suggests that he might be <u>affected</u> by his <u>earlier actions</u> after all.

2) At the end of Act Three, Phil behaves differently towards Leah — he offers her a sweet and puts his arm around her to <u>make amends</u>. An actor might do this <u>tentatively</u> to show he's uncertain of her reaction.

3) When Leah "*Storms off*", Phil breaks his silence to call after her ("Leah? Leah?"). Here, an actor could <u>raise his voice</u> and use a <u>desperate tone</u> to make this outburst even more surprising to the audience.

4) In Act Four, the stage directions say that Phil "*<u>is not eating</u>*". This is <u>unusual</u> for him, so it might be taken as a sign that he feels <u>guilty</u>, or that he <u>misses Leah</u>.

5) Throughout Richard's monologue, an actor playing Phil might <u>stare into the distance</u> with a <u>sorrowful expression</u> — his lip may even tremble to show that Phil is upset and on the verge of <u>crying</u>.

Effect on the Audience

Phil's behaviour at the end of the play adds complexity and depth to his character — the audience are <u>unlikely</u> to <u>forgive</u> his earlier actions, but they might <u>sympathise</u> with his reaction to being <u>rejected</u> by Leah in Act Three.

There's the strong, silent type — and then there's Phil...

In a group, choose one person to be Phil and sit them in the 'hot seat'. Take it in turns to question them — the person in the 'hot seat' must remain in character. You might want to ask:

1) Why did Phil ignore Leah for such a long time?
2) How does Phil feel now that Leah is gone?
3) How does Phil feel about Adam? Why did he arrange to have him killed? Does he regret it?

Imagine this interview is taking place after the events of the play.

Character Performance — Cathy

Cathy isn't the sharpest tool in the shed, but that doesn't make her any less dangerous — more so, if anything. Here's how to make the most of her transformation from fame-seeking teenager to cold-blooded killer.

Cathy is more dangerous than she initially appears

1) Cathy comes across as an <u>amoral character</u> — she doesn't appear to have any understanding of <u>right</u> and <u>wrong</u>. She <u>bullies</u> Brian and Adam, and she's heavily involved in <u>covering up</u> Adam's disappearance.

2) However, Cathy isn't especially <u>intelligent</u>. She <u>blindly follows</u> the leader of the group, whether it's Phil or John Tate. She also puts the cover-up at risk when she thoughtlessly implicates an innocent postman.

3) She becomes more outwardly <u>violent</u> towards the end of the play, which Phil exploits to get her to <u>kill</u> Adam in Act Three. In Act Four, Richard informs Phil that she is <u>terrorising</u> younger children at school.

Cathy is...
excitable: "This is mad, eh?"
foolish: "We got DNA evidence. We did what you said."
violent: "I threatened to gouge one of his eyes out."

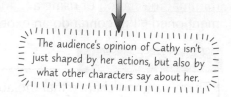

The audience's opinion of Cathy isn't just shaped by her actions, but also by what other characters say about her.

She enjoys taking part in the cover-up...

1) Cathy's "<u>grinning</u>" when she's introduced to the audience in Act One ("*A Wood*"). Her <u>excited reaction</u> to Adam's 'death' presents a <u>striking contrast</u> to the other characters, who are panicking about it.

Here, the actor playing Cathy uses an eager facial expression as John Tate argues with Richard.

2) An actor might say "it's quite exciting as well, though, isn't it" in a <u>light-hearted tone</u> to show that she's <u>untroubled</u> by the serious consequences of the group's actions. This would make her seem <u>heartless</u> in comparison to more agitated characters like Brian.

Physical Skills

- To emphasise Cathy's enthusiasm to the audience, an actor could use <u>animated movements</u> and <u>gestures</u>. She could <u>bounce up and down on her toes</u> to show that she's too excited to keep still.

- Cathy appears to enjoy her role in the cover-up, unlike the rest of the group. An actor might <u>nod enthusiastically</u> while listening to Phil's orders, then <u>move quickly</u> and <u>decisively</u> to carry them out. This would make Cathy stand out from more reluctant characters.

... and tries to use it for personal gain

1) In Act Two ("*A Wood*"), Cathy shows <u>no concern</u> for the man who has been <u>wrongly arrested</u>. Her main focus is the attention that she's receiving from the press — when she tells the rest of the group that she's been asked for an interview, an actor could <u>straighten her clothes</u> or <u>flick her hair back</u>. This would make her seem <u>vain</u> and <u>self-centred</u>.

2) Cathy also mentions the possibility that she'll be paid for speaking to the press — "do you think I should ask for money?" An actor may deliver this line in a <u>loud</u>, <u>high pitched voice</u> and <u>add emphasis</u> to the word "<u>money</u>". This would make it clear that Cathy is <u>excited</u> by the idea of making money from Adam's disappearance.

3) At this point in the play, the rest of the group are discussing the postman that Cathy and Mark framed. An actor playing Cathy might <u>look elsewhere</u> to show that she <u>isn't paying attention</u> — this would reinforce the impression that she only cares about <u>herself</u>.

Character Performance — Cathy

Cathy's capable of extreme violence

1) Cathy becomes <u>increasingly dangerous</u> as the play progresses — she goes from finding Adam's disappearance <u>exciting</u> at the start of the play to committing <u>murder</u> by the end.

2) An actor might choose to hint at Cathy's violent nature throughout the play. For example, she may <u>clench her fists</u> when Danny tells her to "shut up" in Act One ("*A Wood*").

3) In Act Three ("*A Wood*"), Brian says Cathy <u>"loves violence now"</u>, which is confirmed when she "*slaps him*". Here, an actor could put on an <u>angry facial expression</u> and <u>storm towards</u> Brian in a threatening manner. This would make her look <u>more aggressive</u>.

This production showed Cathy and other characters laughing as they bullied Adam.

4) When Phil asks Cathy if she understands that Adam has to die, she responds "Yeah. I do." An actor may deliver this line <u>casually</u> and <u>without hesitation</u> to show that Cathy has no problem killing Adam.

5) The audience doesn't see Cathy suffocate Adam, but an actor might communicate Cathy's determination to do as Phil tells her by <u>moving purposefully</u> and <u>grasping the plastic bag tightly</u> as she leaves the stage.

Effect on the Audience

An actor could show that Cathy <u>enjoys</u> hurting other people. For example, in Act Three ("*A Wood*"), she might have a <u>wide grin</u> on her face and <u>swing</u> the carrier bag to show she is <u>looking forward</u> to <u>killing</u> Adam. Her cheerfulness would be <u>chilling</u> for the audience.

She's in charge at the end of the play

1) Throughout the play, Cathy is drawn to figures of <u>authority</u> like <u>John Tate</u> and <u>Phil</u>. In contrast, she seems to despise <u>weaker</u> characters like Brian. An actor may reflect this in the way she interacts with others:

- An actor might stand in <u>close proximity</u> to the group's leader at the time, maintain <u>eye contact</u> with them and speak to them in a <u>respectful tone</u>. This would suggest that she admires them.
- She may <u>stand further</u> from weaker characters like Brian. She could use a <u>sneering</u> facial expression and adopt a <u>frustrated tone</u> with them, as if she'd rather not talk to them at all.

2) At the end of the play, Richard reveals that Cathy is "<u>running things</u>" — she's <u>taken charge</u> of the group, and it's clear that she's using <u>violence</u> and <u>intimidation</u> to control people.

3) Cathy doesn't appear on stage again after this point, but an actor could use Richard's comment to inform their choice of performance skills earlier in the play. For example, an actor might stand in a <u>centre stage position</u> in earlier scenes to create the impression that she wants to be <u>in control</u> of the rest of the group.

REVISION TASK

Of all the murder weapons to use, she used a bag for life...

Read Act Two ("A Wood") from "We just came from the police station" to "We're screwed". Write a couple of paragraphs about how you would perform Cathy here. You should consider:

1) Your vocal delivery (e.g. volume, pitch, pace, tone).
2) Your use of facial expressions.
3) How you might interact with the other characters, including use of proxemics.

Tick list:
✓ vocal performance
✓ physical performance
✓ interaction between characters

Character Performance — Adam

If you ever think you're having a bad day, just remember Adam. Whether it's eating leaves, stealing vodka, dodging traffic or falling into a massive hole, it's probably safe to say that he's got it worse than you do.

Adam is the group's victim

© Michael Smith/ Auckland Theatre Company

1) Adam is a victim of <u>bullying</u>. He tries to be part of the group, but they take advantage of him by forcing him to perform many <u>risky dares</u>. This leads to a <u>serious accident</u> in which Adam falls down a mineshaft.

2) He only appears on stage once, but the audience finds out about him from <u>other characters</u>. For example, Mark reveals that he's always "<u>hanging around</u>" the group to try and become <u>friends</u> with them.

3) When the audience finally meets Adam, he <u>doesn't fit</u> the description given by the other characters — he's <u>wary</u> of the rest of the group and <u>feels threatened</u> by them rather than wanting to be their friend.

4) Phil orders his <u>murder</u> in order to <u>protect</u> the group.

Adam is...

confused: "I'm... dead?"

bullied: "We got him to eat some leaves."

traumatised: "I couldn't remember anything."

Kelly uses Adam to explore the theme of bullying (see p.10-11).

This actor uses a crouched position to make Adam seem defensive.

He's in a terrible condition

1) Adam is the only character whose <u>appearance</u> is described in any detail — the stage directions say that he looks "*like a tramp*". An actor may communicate his condition to the audience using <u>physical skills</u>:

Physical Skills — Body Language and Movement

- Adam has been <u>missing</u> for several weeks, and he tells the group that he has been living off insects, grass and leaves. An actor may use a <u>huddled posture</u> and <u>bow his head</u> to highlight his <u>weakness</u>. This would also emphasise his <u>vulnerability</u> by making him seem <u>smaller</u> than the rest of the group.

- An actor might use <u>stiff</u> or <u>laboured movements</u> to suggest that Adam is <u>injured</u>. He could <u>wince</u> as he moves to make it clear to the audience that he's <u>in pain</u>.

- The stage directions say that Adam looks like he may "*run off at any moment*". An actor could <u>fidget</u>, <u>shuffle his feet</u> and glance around the stage <u>nervously</u> to create this impression.

2) It needs to be clear to the audience that Adam has been <u>emotionally</u> damaged by his experience and isn't <u>capable</u> of making <u>rational</u> judgements — this will help them <u>understand</u> his decision to return to the hedge instead of going home. An actor's physical performance should reflect Adam's <u>fragile mental state</u> and <u>confusion</u>:

Physical Skills — Facial Expression and Interactions

- An actor might use a <u>glazed facial expression</u> to suggest that Adam isn't paying attention to his surroundings. This could be interpreted by the audience as a sign that he has lost touch with <u>reality</u>.

- When Adam is taken off stage by Brian, an actor might respond <u>calmly</u> and <u>without any resistance</u>. This would suggest that Adam is <u>unaware</u> of Phil's plan to kill him.

Effect on the Audience

Jan and Mark's description of Adam "laughing" and "joking" as they bully him suggests that he's naturally <u>cheerful</u> and <u>friendly</u>. This makes his mental deterioration more <u>striking</u> and increases the audience's <u>sympathy</u> for him.

Character Performance — Adam

He speaks as though he's in shock

1) Adam <u>doesn't speak</u> a lot at the start of Act Three ("*A Wood*") other than to say his name — "Adam, it's Adam, my name's Adam." An actor might deliver this line in a <u>vague</u>, <u>questioning tone</u> to highlight Adam's confusion.

2) However, Adam finally <u>speaks up</u> when Leah asks what happened to him. His monologue presents an actor with another opportunity to reveal Adam's <u>mental state</u> to the audience:

© Helen Murray / ArenaPAL

Vocal Skills

- Adam's speech comes across as incoherent — an actor might use an <u>uneven pace</u> or <u>irregular phrasing</u> to suggest that he's <u>dazed</u> after suffering a head injury in the accident.
- He could <u>pause frequently</u> and <u>scrunch up his face</u> to suggest that he's struggling to recall what happened after the accident.
- Kelly structures Adam's speech by <u>splitting sentences</u> over lines. An actor could use this structure to <u>break up the speech</u> — this would create the impression that Adam is struggling to <u>keep track</u> of what he's saying.

Write about physical and vocal skills in the exam

Take a look at the <u>sample exam</u> answer <u>below</u>. It shows how you could write about performing Adam:

> At the start of Act Three ("*A Wood*"), the stage directions state that Adam "*stands there, twitchily*" whilst the other characters are speaking about him. I would start the scene standing in a centre stage position in the middle of the rest of the group to show that Adam is the centre of attention. To suggest that he is uncomfortable with so much scrutiny, I would shuffle my feet and shift my gaze around the stage, as if searching for an opportunity to escape. Finally, I would speak quietly and use an uncertain tone to say "Adam, my name's, I've got a name, it's..." This would add to the sense that Adam is frightened of the other characters, which would encourage the audience to feel sympathy for him.

This clearly focuses on a <u>specific moment</u>.

This considers how <u>performance</u> could support <u>characterisation</u>.

This explains the <u>effect</u> on the <u>audience</u>.

REVISION TASK

Adam's fear of grilles stopped him cooking that rabbit...

Improvise an imaginary scene in which Adam wakes up after falling into the hole and makes his way back outside. Your performance should consider the following points:

1) Is Adam injured? How could this be shown?
2) What is Adam's mental state at this moment?
3) What is Adam thinking and feeling after the accident? How might these thoughts and feelings be shown to the audience?

Tick list:
✓ physical performance
✓ character's thoughts, feelings and emotions

Character Performance — John Tate

John Tate pops up at the start then disappears into thin air — you'll still need to know all about him, though...

John Tate isn't an effective leader

1) John Tate is the <u>leader</u> of the <u>group</u> at the start of the play — he claims to have improved the other characters' lives, because the rest of the school <u>respects</u> and <u>fears</u> them.

2) He uses <u>intimidation</u> to keep the group in line, but it's clear that he's out of his depth. He gives up his <u>authority</u> to Phil when the <u>pressure</u> of leadership becomes <u>too much</u> for him.

3) He doesn't appear on stage after Act One ("*A Wood*"). Richard says that he has "found god" — this could suggest that he feels <u>responsible</u> for what happened to Adam and wants <u>forgiveness</u> for his part in it.

> John Tate is the only character who's given a surname. This might be interpreted as a sign of his importance.

© Donald Cooper/photostage

John Tate is...

controlling: "No one says that word, okay, no one."

flustered: "I'm finding this all quite stressful."

guilt-ridden: "John Tate hasn't been seen in weeks."

He tries to maintain control...

1) At the start of Act One ("*A Wood*"), John Tate is the <u>dominant</u> figure on stage. An actor might stand in a <u>centre stage position</u> and adopt an <u>upright posture</u> to convey his <u>higher status</u> as the leader of the group.

2) However, John Tate struggles to keep <u>control</u> of the group. Danny and Lou frequently <u>interrupt</u> him at the start of the scene, so he tries to <u>assert himself</u> by banning the word "dead". An actor might speak <u>loudly</u> and <u>emphatically</u> when he tells Richard "do not use that word".

3) He has to <u>defend</u> his <u>position</u> again when Richard stands up to him — as Richard "*steps forward*", John Tate may move to stand in <u>close proximity</u> to him and use <u>aggressive body language</u>, such as prodding Richard in the chest until he backs down.

Physical Skills

An actor could present John Tate as an <u>insecure leader</u> from the start. He could <u>fidget</u> and <u>pace</u> up and down to create this impression.

... but he quickly loses his authority

1) When Phil arrives, John Tate senses an opportunity to shift <u>responsibility</u> onto him — an actor might ask "So. What do we do?" in a <u>pleading tone of voice</u>, as though he's <u>begging</u> Phil to come up with a plan.

2) John Tate doesn't speak again after Phil takes control of the situation — an actor could move into a <u>less prominent</u>, <u>upstage position</u> to emphasise the fact that he's no longer the leader. This would also imply that he doesn't intend to take part in the cover-up and foreshadow his <u>disappearance</u> later in the play.

Effect on the Audience

John Tate's inability to lead the group creates humour in Act One ("*A Wood*"). It's amusing for the audience to watch him become <u>increasingly flustered</u> as he tries to stay in <u>control</u>.

EXAM TIP

There's no sugarcoating it — Tate's an appalling leader...

John Tate only appears on stage for a short time, but you still need to think carefully about the impression you want to create and which performance skills you will use to convey his character to the audience.

Character Performance — Brian

It doesn't take an expert in criminal psychology to figure out that Brian isn't cut out for a life of crime...

Brian isn't as resilient as the others

1) Brian is one of the <u>weakest</u> characters in the group. He bullies Adam along with the others, but he doesn't want to take part in the cover-up. It's only after Phil <u>threatens</u> him that he agrees to lie to the authorities.

2) Brian's state of mind <u>gradually deteriorates</u> over the course of the play. In Act Four ("*A Field*"), Richard says that he's on "stronger and stronger <u>medication</u>" and suggests that he may be sent to a <u>psychiatric hospital</u>.

Brian is...

honest: "I think we should tell someone."

sensitive: "I'm crying because I'm lying and I feel terrible inside."

unstable: "D'you ever feel like the trees are watching you?"

© Hull Truck Theatre

He's a principled character...

1) Brian is introduced to the audience as a <u>vulnerable</u> character — he's "<u>crying</u>" when he enters the stage in Act One ("*A Wood*"). To heighten this effect, an actor might adopt a <u>hunched posture</u>, <u>bow his head</u> and stand towards the <u>edge of the stage</u>. This would also highlight Brian's <u>low status</u> in the <u>group hierarchy</u>.

2) Brian is shocked when he's ordered to lie to the school headmaster. An actor could say "Wha...what?" in a <u>loud</u>, <u>high-pitched voice</u> to suggest that he's horrified by the idea of being dishonest. He doesn't speak for the rest of the scene, so an actor might <u>wring his hands together</u> or <u>shuffle his feet</u> to show his anxiety.

3) He's forced to lie again in Act Two ("*A Wood*") — when he objects, an actor might <u>fold his arms together</u> in an attempt to look <u>more forceful</u>. However, he's <u>terrified</u> of Phil, so an actor might <u>hesitate frequently</u> and <u>stumble over his words</u>. This would show the audience that he's <u>afraid</u> of how Phil will react.

4) Phil <u>frightens</u> Brian into lying to the police by threatening to throw him into the same hole that Adam fell down. At this point, an actor playing Brian may <u>cower away</u> from Phil and <u>shake uncontrollably</u>. This would show that he's <u>scared</u> and make it clear why he <u>gives in</u> to Phil's threats.

> Go back to the plot summary on p.4-5 if you can't remember how or why the cover-up goes wrong.

... who is driven mad by guilt

1) In Act Three ("*A Wood*"), it's immediately obvious that Brian has suffered a <u>mental breakdown</u>. He tries to "*eat a handful of earth*" and "*giggles*" constantly — even when Phil places a plastic bag over his head.

2) To emphasise Brian's mental instability to the audience, an actor could put on a <u>manic facial expression</u> and use <u>erratic movements</u> and <u>gestures</u>. He might <u>approach</u> other members of the group and <u>establish physical contact</u> with them. This would provide a contrast to his <u>introverted behaviour</u> in earlier scenes.

Effect on the Audience

Brian isn't <u>blameless</u> in the group's treatment of Adam, but he's more likely to gain sympathy from the audience than most of the other characters — especially if an actor draws attention to his <u>helplessness</u>.

It's tough, but scoffing dirt isn't going to solve anything...

EXAM TIP Brian isn't the only one to suffer mentally in the play, so you'll need to think of different ways to express emotional turmoil to the audience. A well-rounded performance uses a mix of physical and vocal skills.

Character Performance — Richard

Richard fancies himself as a leader, but he doesn't stand a chance with John Tate and Phil in the picture.

Richard isn't as strong as he thinks

1) Richard falls somewhere in the <u>middle</u> of the <u>group hierarchy</u> — he isn't especially powerful, but he isn't the weakest either.

2) In Act One ("*A Wood*"), the audience learns that Richard tried to become the <u>leader</u> of the group in the past. John Tate dismisses the conflict as "<u>silliness</u>" and says that it's over — it's clear that Richard <u>failed</u>.

3) Richard takes part in the <u>cover-up</u>, but he isn't as involved as some of the other characters. He isn't seen on stage in Act Three, which could suggest that he's trying to <u>distance himself</u> from the rest of the group.

> A character's backstory is a crucial factor in deciding how they should be performed. An actor playing Richard could use his backstory to inform how he might interact with John Tate.

Richard is...

defiant: "You shouldn't threaten me, John."

uneasy: "What if we go to prison?"

forlorn: "Come on, Phil. Come back to us."

He tries (and fails) to assert himself

1) In Act One ("*A Wood*"), Richard hesitantly <u>questions</u> John Tate's leadership. When he warns John Tate against threatening him, an actor playing Richard might <u>draw back his shoulders</u> and <u>stick out his chest</u> to show that he's trying to appear <u>confident</u>.

2) Richard's resistance only lasts for a moment. When John Tate becomes angry, an actor could <u>flinch away</u> from him and use <u>closed body language</u>, as if Richard is frightened of him. To add to this impression, his voice might <u>tremble slightly</u> and <u>trail off towards the end</u> as he says "We are, we are mates now, we —".

3) Richard is a <u>peripheral figure</u> in the group for the rest of Act One. To reflect this, an actor might sit to <u>one side</u> of the other actors and <u>grumble</u> about taking Brian to the headmaster in a <u>quiet voice</u>.

4) Richard <u>complains</u> about his role in the cover-up, but he doesn't defy Phil's orders. In Act Two ("*A Wood*"), an actor might <u>turn his back</u> on the group and <u>fold his arms</u> when they agree to lie to the police. This would express Richard's <u>unwillingness</u> to go along with the plan.

He takes Leah's place in Act Four

1) In Act Four ("*A Field*"), Richard replaces Leah. He desperately seeks Phil's attention and <u>pleads</u> with him to rejoin the group. Here, an actor playing Richard might choose to <u>mirror</u> Leah's <u>physical</u> and <u>vocal performance</u> earlier in the play (see p.26-28).

2) For example, an actor may repeatedly try to <u>make eye contact</u> with Phil while talking to him. He could sit in <u>close proximity</u> to Phil or make <u>physical contact</u> with him to try to get him to reply.

3) An actor might speak at a <u>fast pace</u> and with a <u>nervous tone</u>. This would suggest that Richard is uncomfortable with Phil's <u>passive behaviour</u>, and that he only speaks to <u>fill the silence</u>.

4) Towards the end of the monologue, Richard describes a "vision" that he had on the way to the field — at this moment, an actor may <u>gaze into the distance</u> and speak in a <u>wistful tone of voice</u> to seem <u>thoughtful</u>.

© Hull Truck Theatre

EXAM TIP

I've seen jellyfish with more backbone than Richard...

It's not always easy to tell where characters like Richard fit into the group, so the actors should use stage position and proxemics effectively. This will give the audience a clearer image of each character's status.

Section Three — Character and Performance

Character Performance — Jan and Mark

Jan and Mark don't have a particularly high status in the group, and they do whatever Phil tells them. They're quite happy to cover up Adam's 'death' — as long as it doesn't get them into trouble. Great kids, these two.

Jan and Mark serve as the narrators...

1) Throughout the play, each act starts with a <u>duologue</u> between Jan and Mark in which they introduce the latest <u>plot development</u> for the rest of the act to <u>build on</u>. For example, at the start of Act One, they reveal to the audience that someone is <u>dead</u>. This means that they're like the play's <u>narrators</u> — or a <u>chorus</u>.

2) Jan and Mark constantly <u>interrupt</u> each other, meaning their duologues are delivered at a <u>fast pace</u>. It's important that the actors <u>speak clearly</u> so the audience can understand them.

3) Jan and Mark always appear on stage <u>together</u>, and they don't seem to have many individual characteristics. As a result, the actors may choose to mirror each other's <u>movements</u>, <u>gestures</u> and <u>body language</u>. This would highlight that Jan and Mark are mainly included in the play as <u>plot devices</u> — their role is to <u>hook</u> the audience at the start of each act.

> A plot device is something that's only included in the play to move the plot forwards.

Playwright's Techniques

In <u>Ancient Greek</u> theatre, it was common for plays to include a <u>group</u> of narrators (or a <u>chorus</u>) to comment on the action and provide additional information.

Effect on the Audience

Jan and Mark create <u>suspense</u> for the audience in their scenes on *"A Street"* by only providing them with <u>vague information</u>. The audience are made to <u>wait</u> until <u>later in each act</u> to find out what they're discussing.

... but they're part of the group as well

1) In Act One (*"A Wood"*), Jan and Mark describe Adam's fall. The actors could speak in a <u>dismissive tone</u> to <u>make light</u> of their behaviour ("You know Adam, you know what he's like"). This would make them sound <u>careless</u>.

2) Jan and Mark <u>interrupt each other</u> frequently and <u>hesitate</u> at the start and end of this speech. This suggests that they're <u>uncomfortable</u> describing the group's treatment of Adam. To reflect this, the actors might seek <u>regular eye contact</u> with each other for support.

3) They follow Phil's orders without question, so the actors might <u>respond quickly</u> and <u>nod enthusiastically</u> while Phil is talking.

4) In Act Three (*"A Wood"*), Jan and Mark <u>leave</u> before Phil mentions killing Adam. However, Jan *"thinks"* then *"Nods"* at Mark before they go — this could imply that they're <u>aware</u> of Phil's intentions. To add to this impression, the actors might exit the stage <u>in a hurry</u>. This would show that they want <u>nothing</u> to do with the <u>murder</u>.

Mark and Jan could use excited facial expressions — this would highlight their lack of compassion.

Physical Skills

When Jan and Mark <u>exit</u> in Act Three (*"A Wood"*), they could do so with their <u>heads down</u> to suggest they're trying not to <u>draw attention</u> to themselves. They could <u>pull</u> at each other to suggest they want to get away as <u>quickly</u> as possible.

Name a more iconic duo than Jan and Mark — I'll wait...

EXAM TIP Jan and Mark may not be the most sympathetic of characters, but they provide the actors playing them with a great opportunity to inject some humour. Have a think about how you might do this on stage.

Character Performance — Danny and Lou

Danny and Lou aren't starring roles, but you might regret it on exam day if you haven't revised them...

Danny is a self-interested character

1) Danny seems <u>out of place</u> amongst the rest of the group. The other characters don't appear to care about <u>school</u> or the <u>future</u>, but Danny wants to become a <u>dentist</u>. In fact, he rarely speaks about anything else.

2) He's so determined to become a dentist that he comes across as <u>selfish</u>. For example, his <u>main objection</u> to Adam's 'death' is that it might affect his <u>future career</u> ("Dentists don't get mixed up in things").

Guilt and Responsibility

<u>Minor characters</u> like Danny and Lou aren't as <u>responsible</u> for Adam's death as Phil and Cathy, but they're not <u>guilt-free</u>. It's up to the actors playing them and the director to determine how much of the <u>blame</u> they should receive and how to convey their <u>accountability</u> using performance skills.

3) To express Danny's concern, an actor might <u>fidget nervously</u> and use a <u>worried facial expression</u> when the group discuss the cover-up. He could also speak in a <u>hesitant</u> or <u>trembling voice</u>, as though he's finding it difficult to contain his anxiety.

4) In Act Two ("*A Wood*"), Danny is clearly <u>shocked</u> when Phil threatens Brian. Here, an actor may <u>stare open-mouthed</u> at Phil then say "Is he serious?" in a <u>disbelieving tone of voice</u>.

5) Danny doesn't appear on stage after Act Two, which implies that he's trying to <u>distance himself</u> from the group. An actor might hint at his desire to leave in earlier scenes by standing at the <u>edge of the group</u> and <u>glancing around</u> the stage often.

Effect on the Audience

Danny doesn't contribute much to the <u>main plot</u> — it seems likely that he's included in the play to provide <u>humour</u>, particularly when the audience finds out in Act Four ("*A Field*") that he actually "<u>hates</u>" dentistry.

Lou is nothing more than a follower

1) Lou is an **impressionable** character who seems to be drawn to whoever is **in charge**. She **obeys** John Tate and Phil throughout the play, and Richard reveals that she has become Cathy's "**best friend**" at the end.

2) She readily takes part in the cover-up, although she comes across as **more pessimistic** than the rest of the group. For example, she repeats that they're all "**screwed**" whenever the cover-up encounters **difficulties**.

© Hull Truck Theatre

3) An actor might use **nervous body language** around the other characters to show that Lou is **insecure** about her position in the group. She may also stand in **close proximity** to powerful characters (e.g. Phil), as if she's trying to gain their **approval**.

4) Lou doesn't speak much, but an actor might deliver her lines in an **anxious tone** and add emphasis to the word "**screwed**" whenever she says it. This would make Lou seem **worried**.

5) Unlike Danny, Lou remains part of the group until the end of the play. The stage directions state that she's "**_unsure_**" about leaving Adam with Phil in Act Three ("*A Wood*"), but she leaves after Phil reassures her. An actor could exit the stage **quickly** and **without looking back** to suggest that Lou suspects what will happen to Adam and doesn't want to be involved.

GCSE Drama — it's not quite as painful as pulling teeth...

Kelly doesn't throw minor characters like Danny and Lou into the play at random — everyone is included for a reason. You'll find them easier to write about if you can get your head around why they're on stage.

Practice Questions

After all that, you should know these characters as if they're your best friends. (Actually, forget that. You really don't want to be friends with this lot.) Have a go at these practice questions to check how much you've learnt.

Quick Questions

1) Why doesn't Leah initially object to the plan to cover up Adam's 'death'?

2) Give three moments in the play where Phil shows his authoritative nature.

3) What is Cathy's position in the group at the end of the play?

4) Give two ways that an actor might use physical skills to convey Adam's fear in Act Three.

5) Find one example from the play which shows that John Tate is a weak leader.

6) In Act Two, what makes Brian change his mind and agree to go to the police station?

7) Briefly describe Richard's status in the group.

8) Outline one way in which Jan and Mark act as a chorus in the play.

9) Give two ways that an actor might use vocal skills to portray Danny as nervous in Act One.

10) Outline two character traits that Lou shows in the play.

In-depth Questions

1) Explain how an actor playing Leah could use physical and vocal skills to demonstrate Leah's lack of authority when she is with the group.

2) In the final scene of Act One, Phil ignores Leah. How might an actor use physical skills to show Phil's character in this scene?

3) Explain how an actor might use performance skills throughout the play to convey Cathy's violent nature to the audience.

4) What vocal and physical skills might an actor use to portray Adam as confused in Act Three?

5) How might an actor convey Brian's mental instability in Act Three?

6) Using a combination of physical and vocal skills, how might the actors playing Jan and Mark interact with each other in Act One ("*A Wood*")?

Practice Questions

Time to check that you've got your head around this performance malarkey by having a go at these practice questions. For each one, come up with a brief plan of what you want to cover and then get writing — you should aim for at least three paragraphs per question. On your marks... get set... write.

Exam-style Questions

> Read Act One ("*A Wood*") from Cathy's entrance to where John Tate says "**That just leaves you, Brian**", then answer Question 1 below.

1) Discuss how a performer playing Cathy could communicate key aspects of her character to the audience in this extract. You should consider Cathy's motivations and how the actor could use vocal and physical skills.

> Read Act Two ("*A Wood*") from the point where Richard and Cathy enter to the point where Jan, Mark and Brian enter, then answer Question 2 below.

2) As a performer playing the role of Leah, discuss how you would use performance skills to portray her character in this extract. You should explain why your ideas are suitable for this extract and for the rest of the play.

> Read Act Three ("*A Wood*") from where Leah says "**Phil, what are you doing?**" to the end of the scene, then answer Question 3 below.

3) Imagine you are directing a production of *DNA*. Explain how a performer playing the role of Phil might demonstrate his manipulative personality in this extract and in the play as whole. Refer to vocal skills, physical skills and interactions with other characters.

> Read Act Four ("*A Field*"), then answer Question 4 below.

4) Imagine you're a director creating a production of *DNA*. Discuss how the performer playing Richard might convey his desire to keep the group together, in the extract and the play as a whole. You should consider the performer's use of physical skills, vocal skills and stage space.

Stage Types and Stage Design

A suitable stage type and a well-designed performance space can convey specific ideas to your audience.

'DNA' can be staged in different ways

1) When choosing a stage type, it's important for a director of *DNA* to consider the style of the production.

2) Dennis Kelly intended *DNA* to be open to interpretation (see p.2), so it wasn't written with a particular theatre style in mind. This means that it's up to the director to choose a style and a suitable stage type.

> - A naturalistic production of the play might distance the actors from the audience, e.g. by choosing a stage type that's set back from the audience. This would help to maintain the fourth wall and make the play feel more realistic, which might make it easier for the audience to become immersed in the action on stage.
>
> - A non-naturalistic production might use a stage type that brings the actors and the audience closer together, making it easier for the fourth wall to be broken. This might encourage the audience to reflect on the issues raised by the play by reminding them it's not real life.

The fourth wall is the imagined barrier that separates the audience from the performers.

See p.18 for more on the difference between naturalistic and non-naturalistic theatre styles.

3) The director's choice of performance space needs to be suitable for staging scenes in each of the play's three locations — for example, it needs to be able to convey the confined nature of "A Wood", as well as the more open and public spaces of "A Street" and "A Field".

Different stage types create different effects

There's a glossary on p.72-73 if you're struggling with any of the terms in this section.

1) **Proscenium arch** and **end-on staging** allow the director and designers to use backdrops and larger pieces of scenery without interrupting the audience's line of sight. This makes it easier for them to create a clear and realistic representation of the play's three locations on the stage.

> **Effect on the Audience**
>
> One problem with these stage types is that the audience may be too far away to pick up on some of the actors' performance skills (e.g. facial expressions). This may reduce the emotional impact of the play.

2) **Thrust staging** provides a clear view of the action on stage, because more of the audience are close to the stage and the performers. This might help the audience to develop a deeper emotional connection with the characters at key moments in the play, such as when Leah rejects Phil at the end of Act Three.

3) **Theatre in the round** creates an intimate atmosphere, as the audience completely surrounds the stage. A director could use this stage type to make the performance space feel claustrophobic, particularly in scenes which are set in "A Wood". However, this stage type might cause problems with sightlines and blocking, because the performers will always have their backs to at least one section of the audience.

Theatre in the round can help the audience to feel immersed in the action.

© Helen Murray / ArenaPAL

4) **Traverse staging** creates a similarly intimate atmosphere, and it brings the audience so close together that they can see each other across the stage. This could link to the idea of over-surveillance (see p.6), as it would give the audience a feeling of being watched. However, this stage type limits the amount of scenery and stage furniture that can be used.

5) **Promenade theatre** helps the audience feel more involved in the action. The audience may even start to feel like they're part of the cover-up as they follow the actors between different locations. This would require a large performance space — it might even need to take place outdoors.

Stage Types and Stage Design

Staging and performance space are linked

1) A <u>smaller performance space</u> would create the impression that the actors are <u>crowded together</u> during the three group scenes. This would add to the <u>claustrophobic atmosphere</u> in the wood.

2) In contrast, a <u>larger performance space</u> would allow the actors to spread across the stage more. This would make each actor's <u>actions</u> and <u>reactions</u> easier for the audience to <u>see</u> when there are <u>multiple characters</u> on stage.

3) A director should also consider how <u>different areas</u> of the stage might be used <u>effectively</u>. Stages are often split into <u>nine</u> areas.

4) A director can use actors' stage positions to give the <u>audience</u> clues about characters' <u>status</u>. The audience is likely to pay <u>more attention</u> to characters who are downstage, so they will seem more <u>important</u>. For example, a director might choose to position <u>Phil</u> downstage to reinforce that he is <u>in charge</u>.

Upstage Right (USR)	Upstage Centre (USC)	Upstage Left (USL)
Stage Right (SR)	Centre Stage (CS)	Stage Left (SL)
Downstage Right (DSR)	Downstage Centre (DSC)	Downstage Left (DSL)

AUDIENCE

These positions are used for other staging types as well as proscenium arch — one part of the stage is picked as 'downstage', and this is used as a reference for the other terms.

Entrances and exits can be used for dramatic effect

1) Kelly's stage directions say <u>when entrances</u> and <u>exits</u> occur, but not <u>how</u> or <u>where</u> characters should enter or exit the stage. A director should consider the <u>impact</u> they want each entrance or exit to create.

© Arno Declair

- Jan and Mark <u>interrupt</u> Leah's monologues near the start of the first three acts. The actors playing Jan and Mark might <u>rush on stage</u> via a <u>walkway</u> through the audience at these moments. This would draw the <u>audience's attention</u> to them and make their search for Leah and Phil seem <u>urgent</u>.
- In Act Three ("*A Wood*"), Cathy and Brian move <u>off stage</u> to kill Adam as Leah pleads with them to "stop". Cathy and Brian might exit <u>upstage</u> on the <u>opposite side</u> of the stage to Leah, going <u>down steps</u> into the wings. They would <u>gradually descend</u> out of Leah's (and the audience's) sight, highlighting that Leah can't stop Adam being murdered.

2) The use of entrances and exits also depends on the <u>stage type</u>. For example, <u>theatre in the round</u> could allow numerous entrance and exit points on <u>all sides</u> of the stage. Having characters entering and leaving by <u>different</u> routes would hint that they are <u>detached</u> from one another and are <u>not close</u> friends.

The position of your entrances and exits has to work with the stage type you choose.

REVISION TASK

I have a joke on stage space, but I need longer to planet...

Decide what stage type you would use to produce the final "Field" scene in Act Three. Write two paragraphs about how you would stage this section using this stage type. Write about:

1) Why your choice of stage type is suitable for staging this section.
2) Any disadvantages of using this stage type.
3) The mood and atmosphere you want to create.

Tick list:
- ✓ details about one stage type
- ✓ awareness of practical issues
- ✓ effect on the audience

Set Design

It's not enough for your set design to look nice — it has to reflect the setting and the style of the production.

A naturalistic set is meant to look real...

1) In a <u>naturalistic</u> production of *DNA*, the set design should recreate the play's settings as authentically as possible. This helps the audience <u>suspend their disbelief</u> and become <u>fully immersed</u> in the action.

2) The play could be staged <u>outside</u> in a real street, field and wood. There are <u>practical issues</u> with doing this, so most productions are staged <u>indoors</u>, with a set designed to convey the outdoor settings.

3) For example, the set for "*A Street*" could include a <u>high wall</u> made of polystyrene that has been painted to look like <u>red brick</u> — this would make it look like a generic wall that could be found in any town or city. A designer might choose to cover the wall in <u>graffiti</u> and make it look <u>damaged</u> — this would convey ideas about <u>social responsibility</u> by reminding the audience about anti-social behaviour.

3) The actors playing Leah and Phil could sit together on an <u>artificial grass mat</u> to create a <u>realistic impression</u> of "*A Field*". A set designer might choose to add <u>extra details</u> like <u>plants</u> and <u>bushes</u> for the scenes set in "*A Field*" to make the set more true to life.

4) A realistic representation of "*A Wood*" might be difficult to achieve, but a set designer could use <u>fake trees</u> made of <u>plaster</u> or <u>resin</u>. The trunks might have a <u>rough texture</u> to make them more life-like. To make the set design even more realistic, a designer could scatter <u>real leaves</u> across the stage floor.

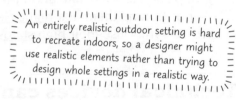

An entirely realistic outdoor setting is hard to recreate indoors, so a designer might use realistic elements rather than trying to design whole settings in a realistic way.

... but it's not the designer's only option

1) In a <u>non-naturalistic</u> production of *DNA*, the set design <u>wouldn't</u> try to recreate real life. <u>Minimalist</u> sets and <u>abstract</u> sets are two ways of achieving a non-naturalistic style.

2) In a <u>minimalist</u> production, the set design doesn't include much in the way of scenery, stage furniture or props, so the design features that are included might have more <u>significance</u>:

- A minimalist set design might communicate each setting to the audience using a <u>single item</u> associated with the setting — e.g. "*A Street*" might be portrayed using a <u>lamppost</u>, while "*A Wood*" might be portrayed using a <u>fallen tree branch</u>.

- These items might be <u>broken</u> in some way to make the set design more <u>symbolic</u>. For example, the street lamp for the "*Street*" scenes may be <u>smashed</u> or <u>rusty</u> to symbolise the <u>breakdown</u> of <u>modern British society</u> (see p.6-7).

3) In an <u>abstract</u> production, the set isn't supposed to look realistic. Using an abstract set design for *DNA* would encourage the audience to <u>think about</u> the <u>themes</u> and <u>issues</u> of the play:

- The scenery in an <u>abstract</u> set might be <u>unrealistic</u> in <u>scale</u> — using <u>oversized</u> scenery would make the group seem <u>smaller</u>, which would emphasise their youth as well as their lack of control over the situation.

- In Act Three ("*A Wood*"), a set designer might replace the trees from previous scenes with others which are <u>gnarled</u> or <u>twisted</u> into unnatural shapes. This would symbolise Adam's and Brian's <u>mental decline</u> and create an <u>unsettling atmosphere</u> for the audience.

This production used a wooden structure to symbolise "A Wood".

© Arno Declair

Section Four — Staging and Design

Set Design

Levels have lots of different uses

1) Kelly's stage directions don't mention stage <u>levels</u>, but a set designer can still use them.

2) Raised platforms (called <u>rostra</u>) could be used to emphasise important moments in the play. In Act Three ("*A Wood*"), Adam might stand on a <u>rostrum</u> in a <u>centre stage position</u>. This would elevate him above the rest of the group and draw the audience's <u>attention</u> to him, increasing the <u>impact</u> of his monologue.

3) A designer could use <u>split staging</u> to show the play's <u>different locations</u> on stage at the <u>same time</u>. Each setting could be on a different level, with settings at the back raised higher than those at the front so the audience could see them all. This would allow the action to switch between a street, a field and a wood without <u>scene changes</u>.

4) Levels can also be used to reveal more about the <u>dynamics</u> of the group. For example, <u>leaders</u> of the group such as John Tate and Phil could stand on rostra — positioning them at a <u>higher level</u> to other characters would symbolise their high <u>status</u>.

> **Split Staging**
>
> A director could also use <u>split staging</u> to show events that occurred <u>before</u> the start of the play. When Jan and Mark describe bullying Adam in Act One ("*A Wood*"), an actor playing Adam could act out what they're describing on a <u>higher level</u> to the rest of the group. This would separate Adam from the others and emphasise that it's a <u>flashback</u>.

Technical devices can make it easier to stage 'DNA'...

1) The play frequently changes location, so technical devices can be used to <u>speed up</u> scene changes and make the transitions <u>smooth</u>. The setting of "*A Street*" could be created by painting a <u>row of houses</u> onto a <u>truck</u>, which could be <u>wheeled away</u> to reveal Phil and Leah sitting behind it for a "*Field*" scene.

© Donald Cooper/photostage

This production projected an image of a wood onto a cyclorama behind the actors.

2) Painted <u>flats</u> could be used to create the effect of different materials. This would allow a set designer to create an impression of <u>heavy</u> or <u>expensive materials</u> like <u>brick</u> or <u>stone</u> without having to use the real thing. This is useful for the play's <u>outdoor settings</u> of the street, field and wood, which contain lots of materials that are difficult to use on <u>stage</u>.

3) A <u>projector</u> could be used to project <u>still</u> or <u>moving</u> images of a street, field or wood onto a cyclorama in an upstage position. This would create a <u>backdrop</u> without needing to build different pieces of <u>scenery</u>, as well as making it <u>quick</u> and <u>easy</u> to swap between the play's <u>three settings</u>.

... and they can also be used to create special effects

A set designer may also use <u>technical devices</u> for <u>dramatic effect</u>, or to enhance the <u>mood</u> and <u>atmosphere</u>:

- In a non-naturalistic production, when Leah talks about "polluting the natural order" in Act Two, images of <u>real newspaper headlines</u> about <u>pollution</u> and <u>global</u> <u>warming</u> could be projected on a screen behind the actors. This would encourage the audience to focus on the <u>environmental issues</u> Leah refers to.

- The <u>entire play</u> takes place <u>outside</u>, so a <u>wind machine</u> might be used to create the impression that the characters' hair and clothes are moving in a breeze. This would make the play's outdoor settings seem <u>more convincing</u> to the audience.

- In Act Three ("*A Wood*"), a <u>smoke machine</u> could be used to release a light mist across the stage. This would create an <u>eerie atmosphere</u>, and it would add to the <u>tension</u> when Adam is taken away by Brian by <u>obscuring</u> their exit from the stage from the audience.

Set Design

Props and stage furniture can be used to create meaning

1) There aren't many moments in the play that require <u>props</u> or <u>stage furniture</u>, but both can still be used to help establish the <u>setting</u>, create <u>symbolism</u> or help with <u>character development</u>.

2) A set designer could use <u>stage furniture</u> to give the audience an <u>impression</u> of the play's settings. For example, "*A Street*" might contain a number of wheelie bins to signify that it's an <u>urban area</u>.

3) <u>Props</u> can be designed to create symbolic effects. For example, Cathy could play with <u>switchblades</u> that increase in size with each act. This would symbolise her <u>increasingly violent nature</u> and create a <u>fearful mood</u>. Phil's plastic bag in Act Three ("*A Wood*") might be <u>red</u> to symbolise its <u>deadly purpose</u> — it's the <u>weapon</u> Cathy uses to <u>murder</u> Adam.

4) Props can also reveal more about a character. For example, a designer could draw the <u>audience's attention</u> to Phil's eating and drinking by using <u>brightly coloured wrapping</u> on his food that is <u>noisy</u> to remove.

Phil (played by a female actor) holds a fizzy drink.

Effect on the Audience

Phil's <u>constant snacking</u> is an important source of <u>humour</u> in the play. A designer should make sure the food props are <u>visible</u> to the audience, so it's clear when they're used.

Explain the ideas behind your set design

When you're writing about set design <u>in the exam</u>, it's important to <u>explain</u> the choices that you've made and their <u>effect</u> on the <u>audience</u>. Here's an example of how you might do this:

> *This shows a good understanding of <u>how</u> technical devices are used.*

>   In Act Two ("*A Street*"), I would construct the scenery using <u>trucks</u> painted to look like red brick walls <u>to reflect the scene's urban setting.</u> The simple set design wouldn't distract the audience and would ensure that their focus remained on Jan and Mark. <u>Jan and Mark's duologue focuses on Brian's refusal to go to the police, which could mean that the group's cover-up fails.</u> To symbolise the potential unravelling of their plans, I would use paint to create the illusion that the walls are crumbling and some bricks are missing, making them appear unstable.

> *This demonstrates awareness of how design choices <u>affect the audience</u>.*

> *Give at least one <u>reason</u> for every part of the design.*

REVISION TASK

The scenery's made of jelly — I'm waiting for it to set...

Imagine you're a set designer for a naturalistic production of 'DNA'. Draw an annotated sketch of your set design, including its position on the stage, for a scene set in "A Wood". Include:

1) The materials, textures and colours that you'd use.
2) Any technical devices that might be needed.
3) A brief explanation of why your design choices are appropriate for a naturalistic production of the play.

Tick list:
✓ specific design details
✓ correct use of technical language
✓ understanding of style

Lighting

Lighting designers use (you guessed it...) lighting to support the action on stage — they're a bright bunch.

The use of lighting depends on the style of the production

1) Lighting designers can change the <u>direction</u>, <u>colour</u> and <u>intensity</u> of lighting to create a range of effects.

2) The lighting for a <u>naturalistic</u> production of *DNA* should make the play's outdoor settings seem <u>realistic</u>. A lighting designer might use lighting effects that mimic <u>natural light</u> like <u>sunlight</u> and <u>moonlight</u>.

3) A naturalistic production could also use visible sources of <u>artificial lighting</u> to reflect the <u>modern setting</u>. For example, a <u>working street light</u> might be used to illuminate Jan and Mark in the "*Street*" scenes.

4) Lighting designers have <u>more freedom</u> in <u>non-naturalistic</u> productions, because the onstage lighting <u>doesn't</u> have to create a <u>realistic impression</u>. For example, when Phil explains his plan to the others during Act One ("*A Wood*"), the light might fade until he is the only character lit by a <u>profile spotlight</u>. This non-naturalistic use of lighting would make him <u>stand out</u> as the group's new <u>leader</u>.

Lighting has a wide range of practical uses

A key concern for a lighting designer is making sure that the audience can <u>see</u> what's happening on stage. However, lighting has other <u>practical</u> uses:

- Lighting can be used to establish the play's <u>settings</u>. For example, a lighting designer might place <u>gobos</u> over the stage lanterns to create a <u>dappled</u>, <u>leafy effect</u> in the scenes that happen in "*A Wood*".

- It can also be used to indicate the <u>time of day</u>. Focusing a light through a <u>yellow gel</u> would create the impression that it's daytime, while using a <u>dark purple gel</u> would show that it's night.

- The colour of the lighting can create an impression of <u>temperature</u>. For example, a <u>broad wash</u> of <u>pale blue light</u> might be used to suggest that it's <u>cold</u> when Phil and Leah are alone together in "*A Field*". This would also highlight Phil's cold treatment of Leah using <u>colour symbolism</u> (see p.49).

This production used gobos to create a dappled lighting effect.

It can be used to support characterisation

1) Designers can use lighting to emphasise the <u>qualities</u> of a particular character. When Phil shows Cathy how to suffocate Adam in Act Three ("*A Wood*"), <u>uplighting</u> could be used to <u>cast shadows</u> over Phil's face and body. This would give him a <u>threatening appearance</u> and hint at his <u>dangerous</u> side.

2) Lighting could highlight a character's <u>position</u> in the group. The group leader at any given moment (e.g. John Tate or Phil) might be <u>brightly illuminated</u> by a <u>sharply-defined</u> beam to emphasise their importance, but other characters (e.g. Brian) might be more <u>dimly lit</u>. This would draw attention to the <u>most authoritative</u> member of the group.

> **Power and Group Dynamics**
>
> The idea of power and authority within the group is a <u>key theme</u> in *DNA*, so it should be explored in detail — this can be done by both the <u>designers</u> and the <u>actors</u>.

3) It can also reveal more about the <u>relationship</u> between different characters. For example, Leah and Phil may be lit by <u>separate spotlights</u> in the scenes that take place in "*A Field*", with the rest of the stage very dimly lit. The <u>darkness</u> between the characters would highlight the <u>emotional distance</u> between them.

Lighting

Lighting can create mood and atmosphere...

1) The <u>colour</u> of lighting can have a major impact on the <u>mood</u> and <u>atmosphere</u> of the play — it can provide the audience with a visual representation of how the characters are <u>feeling</u>. For example, in Act Four ("*A Field*"), the lighting might be <u>dimmer</u> and have <u>colder tones</u> than in previous "*Field*" scenes. This would help to create a <u>gloomy mood</u> that would reflect Phil's <u>unhappiness</u> after Leah has left.

2) A lighting designer might use colour <u>symbolically</u>. For example, <u>red light</u> may be cast across the stage using <u>red gels</u> to symbolise <u>danger</u> when Phil threatens to kill Brian in Act Two ("*A Wood*").

© Helen Murray / ArenaPAL

> ### Colour Symbolism
>
> Colour symbolism uses the <u>feelings</u> and <u>ideas</u> that are associated with certain <u>colours</u> to create <u>meaning</u> for the audience. It's mainly used in <u>non-naturalistic</u> productions and isn't limited to <u>lighting</u> — it could also be applied to other design elements, such as <u>set design</u> and <u>costume</u>.

3) The <u>intensity</u> of lighting can help to build tension. When John Tate threatens Richard in Act One ("*A Wood*"), a <u>parcan</u> could be used to cast an <u>intense beam</u> on Richard <u>from above</u>. This would highlight the <u>pressure</u> that Richard is feeling and add to the <u>tension</u> as the audience wonders how the conflict will be resolved.

... and heighten the impact of key moments

1) Special lighting effects can be created to increase the impact of certain moments. For example, <u>strobe lighting</u> could be used when Adam describes his fall to the rest of the group. This would have a <u>disorientating effect</u> on the audience, and would reflect how <u>confused</u> and <u>upset</u> Adam feels.

2) When Leah talks to Phil about "déjà vu" at the end of Act Two, she may be lit by a <u>Fresnel spotlight</u> with a <u>softly-defined</u>, <u>pale yellow beam</u>. This <u>slightly hazy lighting</u> would create a <u>surreal effect</u> that would link to Leah's comment that "reality is not what we think".

3) An <u>absence of light</u> can also be <u>effective</u> in supporting the action of the play. For example, a <u>blackout</u> could be used when Phil puts a plastic bag over Brian's head in Act Three ("*A Wood*"). This would allow the audience to <u>experience</u> what Brian is going through. It would also <u>avoid</u> the actor playing Brian having a bag over his head for a prolonged period, which could be <u>unsafe</u>.

> ### Effect on the Audience
>
> A <u>blackout</u> would create <u>tension</u>, as the audience would only know that Brian is <u>alive</u> thanks to his speech and the sound of his giggling.

REVISION TASK

How many designers does it take to change a lightbulb...*

Choose one of the "Field" scenes from the play. Make a list of all of the lighting techniques you would use in that scene, and the effects you want to create. You should cover the following:

1) The lighting equipment you would use.
2) The colour, direction and intensity of the lighting.
3) Any special lighting effects that might be created and how, as well as their desired effect on the audience.

Tick list:
- ✓ technical terminology
- ✓ specific design details
- ✓ effect on the audience

*None — isn't that a technician's job?

Sound

If you hold these pages to your ear, you might hear the sea. Though reading them might be more useful...

A sound designer should consider the director's vision

1) Kelly doesn't include much information about sound in the stage directions — he indicates when there should be "*silence*" on stage, but he doesn't refer to any music or sound effects.

2) Although this means that a sound designer can be creative, it's important that all sound effects are in keeping with the director's vision and the overall style of the production.

3) When a designer makes a sound plot, they need to consider how sound can:

- convey the setting and context
- convey actions on and off stage
- emphasise characterisation
- create mood and atmosphere

A sound plot is a plan that contains a list of all the sounds and sound equipment used for a production. It also says when each sound should be used.

Sound can establish the play's settings...

1) The action takes place in three outdoor settings — a sound designer might create a different soundscape for each one. For example, the bustling atmosphere of a 21st-century "*Street*" might be created with pre-recorded sounds like distant traffic noise and sirens, the sound of a dog barking and a radio playing.

A soundscape is created by layering up sounds — this can give a strong sense of place.

2) In "*Field*" scenes, a soundscape of occasional birdsong, a gentle breeze rustling through grass and trickling water might be used to create a peaceful impression. This would make this setting feel open and spacious, as well as showing that Leah and Phil are distanced from the other settings and the rest of the group.

3) A sound designer might use pre-recorded sounds, such as twigs snapping or leaves rustling, in the scenes that occur in "*A Wood*". These sounds could be routed through speakers positioned around the audience — this use of surround sound would make the setting more vivid to the audience.

... and support the action of the play

1) A sound designer can use live sound effects to emphasise onstage actions. For example, the rustling sound of the packaging from Phil's snacks might be captured by an overhead microphone. This would draw the audience's attention to Phil's eating and away from what Leah is saying to him during "*Field*" scenes, emphasising how little attention Phil pays to Leah.

© Helen Murray / ArenaPAL

2) Other sound effects might be created off stage to suggest that the action is happening elsewhere. In Act One ("*A Wood*"), the audience might hear Brian "*crying*" through a speaker before he appears on stage.

3) Sound can also be used to highlight the importance of an action. For example, a sound designer might use a pre-recorded sound of footsteps on leaves when Adam is led away in Act Three ("*A Wood*"). This sound might get quieter as he gets further away to emphasise to the audience that he isn't coming back.

The sounds described on this page are all diegetic. This means the characters on stage can hear them and that they form part of the action, rather than being there to create mood.

Characterisation

A sound designer might use wireless microphones to amplify the actors' voices differently. For example, the speech of dominant characters like John Tate or Phil might be amplified more than the rest of the group — this would emphasise their authority over the other, weaker characters.

Sound

Incidental music can add to the mood and atmosphere...

A sound designer can use <u>incidental music</u> to create or enhance <u>mood</u> and <u>atmosphere</u>:

Incidental music is non-diegetic — the characters can't hear it.

© Arno Declair

- During Act Three ("*A Wood*"), <u>low-pitched string instruments</u> could be played in a <u>minor key</u> for a few seconds when Cathy and Brian leave the stage. This would create a <u>threatening atmosphere</u> and suggest to the audience that Cathy is going to go through with murdering Adam.

- The scenes set in "*A Field*" could be <u>underscored</u> with <u>soft piano music</u> to highlight the <u>decreased tension</u> in this setting. In contrast, this music might increase in volume and become <u>discordant</u> during <u>more violent</u> moments, like when Leah tries to strangle herself in Act One.

Underscoring is when incidental music plays softly in the background to accompany the action or create a certain mood or atmosphere.

... as can other non-diegetic sounds

Incidental music isn't the only type of <u>non-diegetic sound</u> that a sound designer could use:

1) <u>Cellos</u> might be used to create <u>low</u>, <u>rumbling</u> sounds to announce Phil's arrival on stage in Act One ("*A Wood*"). This would highlight Phil's <u>importance</u> and build <u>anticipation</u> for what will happen next.

2) A <u>timpani</u> or <u>bass drum</u> could be played live in the wings to create <u>ominous sound effects</u> which echo around the stage. This may be used at the end of Act Three ("*A Wood*") when Leah pleads with Phil not to kill Adam. This would add to the <u>tension</u> and emphasise the <u>fearful mood</u>.

3) Sound effects can be used for <u>comic effect</u>. For example, <u>cymbals</u> or <u>bar chimes</u> could over-dramatise Leah's attempt to predict the future in "*A Field*" at the end of Act Two, making her failure <u>funnier</u>.

Be specific about sound in the exam

When you're writing about sound <u>in the exam</u>, you should make it clear <u>how</u> and <u>when</u> each sound is made:

Describe the sounds you would use as <u>clearly</u> as possible.

At the beginning of Act One ("A Wood"), I would establish the play's setting by using a pre-recorded soundscape of trees creaking in the wind, crows cawing and bushes rustling. This would make the setting seem creepy and reinforce the ominous atmosphere established in the previous scene. I would position speakers around the audience to create surround sound, so they would be immersed in this setting. The sounds would fade when the characters start speaking to stop the audience being distracted by the sound effects.

Use <u>technical terms</u> to explain your ideas to the examiner.

Remember to write about the effect on the <u>audience</u>.

EXAM TIP

The end of these pages must be like music to your ears...

It's important that you don't lose sight of the bigger picture when you're writing about sound design in the exam. All of your ideas should work together and contribute to the overall style of the production.

Costume

There's much more to costume design than dressing all of the characters in the same ol' school uniform.

Realistic costumes reflect the play's context

1) All the characters in *DNA* are school pupils, so in a <u>naturalistic</u> production a costume designer might convey the play's 21st-century setting by dressing the group in <u>modern school uniform</u>.

2) For example, the group could wear <u>white button-up shirts</u> along with <u>grey trousers</u> or <u>skirts</u> made from materials such as <u>polyester</u> which are commonly used in the 21st century. The costumes might include <u>ties</u> and <u>blazers</u>, which could <u>match</u> in <u>colour</u> and <u>pattern</u> to suggest that the characters attend the <u>same school</u>.

© Donald Cooper/photostage

A costumer designer has to consider details including the material, colour, style, fit and condition of every item of clothing.

Costume design can be used to support the action...

1) A costume designer can use <u>clothing</u>, <u>hair</u> and <u>make-up</u> to reinforce what's happening in the play.

2) When Jan and Mark interrupt Leah at the end of a *"Field"* scene, they might appear <u>sweaty</u> and have <u>messy</u> clothing and hair. This would make it seem like they have been <u>running</u> to find Leah and Phil.

3) In Act One (*"A Wood"*), a costume designer could apply make-up around Brian's eyes so they look <u>red</u> and <u>swollen</u>. This would suggest that he's been <u>crying</u> for a long time before appearing on stage.

4) Leah might wear a <u>coat</u> and a <u>scarf</u> when she threatens to leave Phil near the start of Act Three, as though she's trying to convince him that she's <u>serious</u> about <u>leaving</u>.

Effect on the Audience

A character's costume can effect the <u>audience's opinion</u> of that character. For example, the audience is likely to have more <u>sympathy</u> for Brian if he looks like he's been crying.

A costume designer should make sure costumes are practical for the actors to wear. They need to be comfortable and safe, and shouldn't restrict an actor's movements or actions.

... and it can reveal information about the characters

1) Given that all the characters might be wearing a <u>similar</u> school uniform, a costume designer might want to include <u>individual details</u> in each costume to reveal more about each character's <u>personality</u>:

- Phil's clothing and hair might be <u>clean</u> and <u>neat</u> to match his <u>calm</u> and <u>collected</u> <u>behaviour</u>. However, he might wear <u>trainers</u> and a <u>hoodie</u> instead of smart shoes and a blazer to show that he doesn't <u>conform</u> to society's expectations.

- Cathy's costume could be used to suggest she's <u>unpredictable</u> and doesn't follow rules. She might wear an <u>untucked shirt</u> with an <u>open collar</u>, wear a lot of <u>make-up</u> and have multiple <u>piercings</u> to reflect her <u>rebellious</u> side.

- Brian is more <u>well-behaved</u> than the rest of the group, so he might wear a <u>smarter uniform</u> and style his hair into a <u>neat side parting</u>. This would show his desire to follow the rules.

These are just examples. The idea of tweaking a character's costume to match their personality can be applied to every character in the play.

2) A character's costume might be used to convey their <u>position</u> in the group. For example, Phil's costume could be <u>more individual</u> to set him apart from the group, while <u>lower-status characters</u> such as Danny and Lou could wear the <u>same costume</u> to reflect that they're part of a group following a leader.

Costume

A character's costume might change during the play

1) A costume designer can use <u>changes</u> in costume to reinforce a <u>character arc</u> to the audience.

2) For example, Brian's appearance may become <u>progressively worse</u> as the play goes on. At the start of the play, he could look <u>clean</u> and wear <u>tidy clothing</u>. In Act Three ("*A Wood*"), make-up could be used to make him look <u>filthy</u>, and his clothes could be <u>mismatched</u> and <u>untidy</u>. This would give the audience a <u>visual representation</u> of his <u>mental decline</u> and encourage them to feel <u>more sympathy</u> for him.

3) Phil could have <u>fashionable</u>, <u>neat</u> clothing and hair in the first three acts of the play. Then, in Act Four, his costume could become <u>messier</u> to suggest that he isn't <u>taking care</u> of his <u>appearance</u> anymore. This would reinforce to the audience that he's <u>miserable</u> about Leah leaving.

Costumes can be non-naturalistic

1) In a <u>non-naturalistic</u> production, the costumes could reflect the play's <u>themes</u> or have <u>symbolic meaning</u>.

This production dressed the characters in red, which could symbolise blood and violence.

2) A costumer designer could dress the group in <u>orange boiler suits</u> to make them look like <u>prisoners</u>. This would highlight that they are behaving like <u>criminals</u>, and also increase the tension by acting as a visual reminder of what might happen to them if they're caught. Individual details could show each character's <u>personality</u> — e.g. Cathy's costume might be <u>ripped</u> to suggest that she's been in a fight.

3) Alternatively, some characters could be dressed in <u>different colours</u> to show their personalities using <u>colour symbolism</u>. For example, Leah may wear <u>white</u>, which is associated with <u>goodness</u> and <u>innocence</u>, to suggest she's not as <u>guilty</u> as the other characters.

4) In a <u>minimalist</u> production, all the characters might be dressed in <u>plain</u>, <u>black clothing</u>, except for the group leader. This would highlight the <u>mob mentality</u> of the group, making it harder for the audience to distinguish the characters from one another.

Justify your costume choices in the exam

Here's an example of how you could write about <u>Adam's</u> costume:

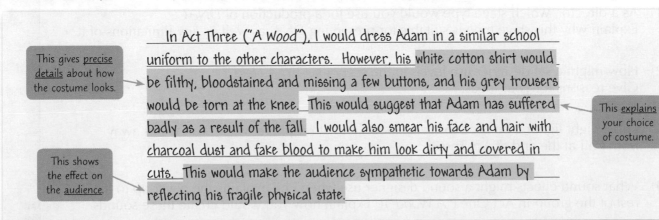

This gives <u>precise details</u> about how the costume looks.

This <u>explains</u> your choice of costume.

This shows the effect on the <u>audience</u>.

> In Act Three ("A Wood"), I would dress Adam in a similar school uniform to the other characters. However, his white cotton shirt would be filthy, bloodstained and missing a few buttons, and his grey trousers would be torn at the knee. This would suggest that Adam has suffered badly as a result of the fall. I would also smear his face and hair with charcoal dust and fake blood to make him look dirty and covered in cuts. This would make the audience sympathetic towards Adam by reflecting his fragile physical state.

EXAM TIP

I'm not going to dress it up — costume design is tricky...

If you're answering a question about costume design, don't forget that a character's costume goes beyond the clothes that they're wearing — it's just as important to think about details like hair and make-up.

Practice Questions

The stage is set, the path to success is lit, you can hear the end of the section calling and you're dressed to impress. It's time to bring it all together with some practice questions, so see how you get on with this lot.

Quick Questions

1) Give two factors that directors must take into account when choosing a stage type for a production of *DNA*.

2) Give one reason why a set designer might choose a non-naturalistic set design for *DNA*.

3) Explain two ways that technical devices such as trucks, flats or projectors could make it easier to stage *DNA*.

4) How might a designer use lighting to reveal more about a specific character's personality?

5) What is colour symbolism? Give an example of how it could be used for effect when lighting a production of *DNA*.

6) Why might a sound designer for *DNA* amplify one character's voice more than others?

7) Give one example of how non-diegetic sound could be used in *DNA* to create a fearful mood.

8) Give three examples of details a costume designer has to consider when creating an item of clothing.

9) How might a designer use costume to reflect a character's position in the group?

In-depth Questions

1) As a director, which stage type would you use for a production of *DNA*? Explain why this stage type is suitable for presenting *DNA*, as well as any limitations of it.

2) How might a set designer use levels in the scenes set in *"A Field"*? Give reasons for your ideas.

3) How might lighting be used to create mood and atmosphere when Leah walks away from Phil at the end of Act Three?

4) What sound effects might a sound designer use when Phil explains the cover-up to the rest of the group in Act One (*"A Wood"*)? Explain how you would create these sounds.

5) Explain how a designer could use costume to show that Cathy is dangerous. You might want to suggest how this costume would change as the play goes on.

Practice Questions

Now you know how to design a production, you need to practise designing the perfect answer to some exam questions. When you're finished, why not treat yourself to an ice cream... or a packet of crisps... or a waffle?

Practice Questions

> Find the part of Act One where Leah and Phil are introduced to the audience for the first time. Read from where it says "**LEAH and PHIL, PHIL eating an ice cream**" to where it says "**JAN and MARK enter**", then answer Question 1 below.

1) Imagine you're a designer working on *DNA*.
   Explain how you would use staging and set design to portray this extract effectively on stage to the audience. You should refer to the play's context in your answer.

> Read Act One ("*A Wood*") from the start to "**This is mad, eh?**", and then answer Question 2 below.

2) Imagine you're a costume designer working on staging this extract of *DNA*.
   Describe how you would use costume design to enhance the production of this extract and the play as a whole on the audience.

> Read Act Two ("*A Street*") from where Jan says "**What?**" to where she says "**What are we going to do?**", then answer Question 3 below.

3) Imagine you're a lighting designer working on *DNA*.
   Describe how you would use lighting design to enhance the impact of the play on the audience in this extract and the play as a whole.

> Read Act Four ("*A Field*") from where it says "**RICHARD sits with PHIL**" to the end of the scene, then answer Question 4 below.

4) Imagine you're a sound designer working on staging this extract of *DNA*.
   Explain how you would use sound design to portray this extract effectively on stage to the audience. You should refer to mood and atmosphere in your answer.

Act One

This section looks at performance skills and design features using the kind of close analysis you should be doing in the exam — excited yet? If you want a reminder of the plot, look back at the introduction (p.4-5).

Act One creates a mood of anxiety

1) Act One plays an important role in establishing the <u>mood</u> and <u>atmosphere</u> of the play — there are <u>humorous</u> moments, but these are overshadowed by the dominant mood of <u>fear</u> and <u>unease</u>. The act also <u>introduces</u> the <u>characters</u> and shows the <u>relationships</u> between them.

2) The play opens with Mark telling Jan that someone is <u>dead</u> — this creates <u>suspense</u> and establishes a <u>tense mood</u> as the audience waits to find out <u>who</u> has died and <u>how</u> the characters are involved.

3) The action moves to "*A Field*", where Leah talks to Phil. The <u>contrast</u> between Phil's silence and Leah's chattiness is initially <u>funny</u>. However, Phil's silence becomes <u>unnerving</u>, especially when Leah tells him she's scared — this creates <u>tension</u> as it makes the audience <u>wonder</u> why she's afraid.

4) In the next scene, John Tate tries to assert his <u>authority</u> over the group but shows himself to be a <u>weak leader</u>. This scene establishes the characters' <u>personalities</u> and <u>relationships</u>, whilst adding to the <u>fearful</u> mood.

5) The mood <u>darkens</u> further when Jan and Mark describe <u>Adam's fall</u> down the mineshaft. The details of the <u>bullying</u> and their attempts to deny responsibility create an <u>unsettling</u> atmosphere.

6) The <u>anxious</u> mood continues to the end of Act One. The audience is left <u>guessing</u> whether Phil's plan to cover up Adam's 'death' will work, and Leah's statement that the group are in <u>trouble</u> heightens the <u>ominous mood</u> going into the second act.

Phil has a focused facial expression as Mark describes Adam's fall.

© Donald Cooper/photostage

Leah reveals her insecurities

See p.26-28 for more ideas on how to perform the character of Leah.

1) Act One ("*A Field*") is the <u>first impression</u> the audience get of Leah's and Phil's characters and relationship.

2) Leah's monologue reveals her lack of self-confidence and desire for <u>understanding</u> and <u>reassurance</u> from Phil. An actor playing Leah could show how she feels using <u>performance skills</u>:

Physical Skills — Movement and Proxemics

- An actor could use <u>movement</u> and <u>proxemics</u> to show how Leah is feeling. When she says "Not that I'm bothered", she could <u>move away</u> from Phil to show she's <u>embarrassed</u>. When she "*sits*", she could leave a <u>gap</u> between her and Phil to highlight the emotional <u>distance</u> between them. Later in the monologue, when she admits to being "scared", she could <u>move closer</u> to Phil as if she is seeking <u>reassurance</u>.

- As Leah talks about fear, she could move round to <u>face</u> Phil — this would show her desire for <u>closeness</u> and <u>comfort</u> from him.

- Leah could <u>fidget</u> to show that she feels <u>anxious</u> — she might <u>wring her hands</u> or keep <u>shifting</u> her position to show that she is uncomfortable and self-conscious.

Vocal Skills — Volume, Emphasis and Pace

- An actor playing Leah could <u>speak loudly</u> when she says "I'm not bothered, Phil" to show that she is <u>pretending</u> to be <u>confident</u>. This could contrast with a <u>quiet delivery</u> of lines such as "Everyone's scared. S'not just me" to show her <u>real</u>, <u>vulnerable</u> self.

- She could <u>stress</u> words such as "scared" and "terror" to emphasise her fear.

- When Leah talks about the fact that she "talks too much", she could speak <u>quickly</u> as if the words are tumbling out — this could suggest that Phil's silence makes her <u>nervous</u>.

- Leah could <u>trail off</u> on sentences that end with an ellipsis, such as "You need me as much as..." to suggest that she <u>doesn't really believe</u> what she's saying.

Act One

John Tate tries to control the group

1) In Act One ("*A Wood*"), John Tate tries to assert his authority over the group, but in doing so shows he is <u>scared</u> of losing control. The actors could use <u>performance skills</u> to show their status:

Physical Skills — Movement

- John Tate could <u>pace</u> around the stage to show that he's anxious about losing his power over the group. When Richard stands up to John Tate and says that he "shouldn't threaten" him, John Tate could <u>puff his chest</u> out and <u>stride confidently</u> up to Richard to show he wants to intimidate him.
- When each character confirms they are on John Tate's "side", they could physically move to <u>stand next</u> to him, possibly with their head lowered to show their obedience to him.
- When Phil enters, he could move to centre stage while John Tate <u>moves swiftly</u> to one <u>side</u>. This would imply that John Tate wants <u>Phil</u> to <u>take control</u> of the group.

2) At this point in Act One, the audience are forming their <u>first impressions</u> of the rest of the group. The actors' <u>costumes</u> help to shape the audience's <u>initial reaction</u>:

Costume Design — Clothing and Accessories

The characters could wear <u>school uniforms</u> to reflect their age. However, subtle differences and additions can hint at one aspect of a character's <u>personality</u> and <u>status</u> in the group. For example:

- Danny could wear glasses and a neat uniform to suggest he is <u>studious</u>.
- Brian could wear clothes that are <u>out of fashion</u> and differ slightly from everyone else's to highlight that he is an <u>outsider</u>. For example, Brian could wear a <u>poorly fitting school blazer</u> while the others wear <u>fashionable jackets</u>.
- John Tate could have a <u>cigarette</u> behind his ear and an untucked shirt to show he is a <u>rebel</u>.

Jan and Mark describe Adam's fall down the mineshaft

1) Jan and Mark's account of what happened to Adam creates a <u>tense</u> and <u>unsettling</u> atmosphere as they gradually reveal the <u>increasingly brutal</u> details of their bullying. <u>Lighting</u> could be used to focus the audience's attention on the pair's growing <u>guilt</u> as they describe their actions.

2) A profile <u>spotlight</u> could be trained on Jan and Mark to show that the group's attention is on them. The light could gradually grow <u>brighter</u> to draw attention to their <u>uncomfortable</u>, <u>guilty</u> facial expressions.

3) After Jan says she "went home", the spotlight beam could <u>narrow</u> around Mark to <u>isolate</u> him from the rest of the group.

4) <u>Floodlights</u> rigged above the performance space could light the <u>entire stage</u> as John Tate says "Dead. He's dead". This would show that the group's attention is no longer on Mark and would refocus the audience on the group's <u>present situation</u>.

© Helen Murray / ArenaPAL

Physical Skills — Proxemics

- Jan and Mark could <u>stand together</u> at the start of their duologue to show their <u>close relationship</u>.
- When Jan says she "went home", she could <u>move away</u> from Mark to show she is <u>distancing</u> herself from the responsibility for Adam's fall.
- The rest of the group could <u>stand away</u> from the pair to disassociate themselves from Adam's fall. The actor playing John Tate could emphasise this by <u>looking away</u> when Jan and Mark say his name.

Act One

Phil devises a plan to cover up the truth about Adam

1) As Phil outlines his plan, his <u>leadership</u> and the other characters' <u>reactions</u> to his plan could be shown through <u>movements</u> and <u>facial expressions</u>.

2) The stage directions indicate <u>silence</u> before Phil's speech, which could be used to create <u>anticipation</u> about what will happen next. The actor playing Phil could put his drink down slowly to draw the <u>audience's attention</u>.

© Donald Cooper/photostage

3) Phil could use <u>decisive</u> hand gestures, such as <u>pointing</u> when giving instructions like "enter the woods from the south entrance", to show his authority. He could also <u>close his eyes</u> and <u>frown</u> when he is interrupted to show he is concentrating on his plan.

Theatrical Conventions

The scene could end with a <u>tableau</u> where all the characters except Phil <u>freeze</u> as Phil picks up his drink. This would emphasise the <u>importance</u> of the moment by fixing it in the audience's minds as the point where the cover-up begins.

4) Characters like Richard and Danny, who are given instructions they don't like, could <u>clench their fists</u> or <u>scowl</u> to indicate their <u>annoyance</u>. They could quickly go back to <u>listening intently</u> with their arms folded to suggest they're still not happy but have accepted Phil's decision. This would show how strong Phil's <u>control</u> is — Richard and Danny <u>can't oppose</u> him for too long.

5) An actor playing Cathy could show her enjoyment of the situation by <u>smiling slyly</u> and <u>nodding enthusiastically</u>. This would hint at her <u>lack of morals</u> and her desire to please whoever is in charge.

Leah attempts to strangle herself

1) Leah's monologue emphasises her <u>desperate need</u> for Phil's <u>attention</u> — she's even prepared to <u>hurt</u> herself to get it. Lighting can be used to set the mood throughout the scene.

2) Immediately before Leah starts to strangle herself, <u>soft white</u> light could be used to create a <u>gentle mood</u>. This would make Leah's sudden action more <u>shocking</u> as she *"grabs her throat"*.

3) At this point, the white lights could cut out and be replaced by a spotlight focused through a <u>red gel</u>. The red light would make the scene more <u>intense</u>, and <u>colour symbolism</u> would reflect the <u>danger</u> Leah is in. When she *"stops"*, the red light could fade and the white lights come back up to show the danger's <u>over</u>.

4) As Leah says "We're in trouble now", the white stage lighting could start to <u>fade</u> to create a <u>foreboding</u> atmosphere going into the next act.

Set Design — Scenery and Staging

- Images of different weather conditions could be projected onto a <u>cyclorama</u> upstage to reflect different moods, e.g. <u>clear blue skies</u> could be replaced by <u>dark clouds</u> when Leah threatens to kill herself.

- <u>Trucks</u> painted with <u>dark</u>, <u>lifeless bushes</u> and <u>trees</u> could be positioned behind the actors. This would act as a <u>visual reminder</u> of the forest and the cover-up, giving a <u>darker edge</u> to the scene.

- A wooden box covered in hay to look like a <u>hay bale</u> could form a <u>raised platform</u> stage right. Leah could use this as a <u>stage</u> when she strangles herself, reinforcing that she's doing it to get Phil's <u>attention</u>.

- During her monologue about bonobos, Leah could stand on the outer ring of a <u>revolving stage</u>, while Phil sits on the stationary inner ring. Leah's <u>orbit</u> around Phil would reflect the way her life <u>centres</u> on him and how important he is to her.

EXAM TIP

Leah is so into Phil — he leaves her breathless...

The decisions made by the director, actors and designers have an impact on the mood and atmosphere. Consider the overall effect you want to create before settling on any performance or design ideas.

Act Two

Four days have passed since Act One and Phil's plan is working perfectly — no one has any clue where Adam is, and the group are getting along nicely. I imagine things go really well from here. (They do not.)

Act Two gives the group a moral dilemma

1) Things get more <u>complicated</u> in Act Two as the group hear about the postman's arrest. Their varying reactions to this and the resulting arguments allow a director to explore some of the play's <u>themes</u>.

2) Lou, Danny and Leah are <u>panicky</u> and <u>confused</u> about why the postman has been arrested, until Cathy reveals that she got DNA from someone who matched the description Phil made up. This news creates a <u>moral dilemma</u> because the group have to decide whether to save themselves or the postman.

3) Brian <u>refuses</u> to identify the postman — the fact that he stands up to the group shows how desperate he is. Phil <u>threatens</u> to throw Brian down the mineshaft if he doesn't lie — Phil's brutal threat and Brian's terror highlight Phil's <u>power</u>.

4) The act ends with Leah talking about déjà vu and <u>change</u>. This scene creates opportunities for <u>humour</u>, but concludes with Phil's refusal to accept that the world can be changed — this creates a sense of <u>hopelessness</u> going in to Act Three.

The characters' body language shows their different reactions to the postman's arrest.

> Déjà vu is when you feel like you've done or seen something before.

The group find out the postman has been arrested

1) The group are <u>frantic</u> as they learn that a postman is in custody for kidnapping Adam. This is already a <u>tense moment</u>, but its impact on the audience can be <u>enhanced</u> through the use of <u>sound</u>.

2) <u>Diegetic</u> sounds like <u>bird song</u> could be used to make the setting of the wood more vivid for the audience. These sounds could <u>stop abruptly</u> when the characters start arguing. A sound effect of <u>wind whistling</u> through trees could be played to highlight the breaks in dialogue and add to the <u>fearful mood</u>.

3) Kelly uses <u>beats</u> and <u>pauses</u> to indicate when important information about the postman's arrest has been revealed or is about to be revealed. <u>Non-diegetic</u> sound such as a <u>low drum beat</u> could mark each of these moments to build the audience's sense of <u>anticipation</u>.

4) <u>Ominous string music</u> could be played live to highlight the <u>trouble</u> the group are in — the music could start quietly and gradually get <u>louder</u>, cutting out suddenly when Leah says the group may be "a little bit, well, screwed." This would emphasise Leah's line and the group's <u>seemingly impossible</u> situation.

Set Design — Scenery

- A <u>projection</u> of towering trees upstage could make the actors look small in comparison to their surroundings. This would reflect how the group use the wood to <u>hide</u> from society. It could also suggest how <u>powerless</u> the group are to stop events from spiralling out of control after they make the initial decision to cover up Adam's 'death'.

- A designer could dress some scaffolding in <u>camouflage netting</u> to make it look like a wood — the tangled netting would create a sense that the characters feel <u>trapped</u> and <u>unable to escape</u> their situation. Characters could rustle through this netting as they enter — this would create <u>tension</u> as the characters on stage <u>turn nervously</u> to see who is coming.

- <u>Colour symbolism</u> could be used to convey meaning — <u>brown</u>, <u>dying leaves</u> scattered across the stage could represent <u>death</u> and <u>decay</u> and add to the fearful mood.

Act Two

Phil threatens to throw Brian down the mineshaft

1) Brian refuses to go to the police and identify the postman. Knowing that this could jeopardise the cover-up, Phil <u>threatens</u> him. Actors could highlight Phil's <u>power</u> over Brian using <u>physical skills</u>.

2) When Phil *"walks over"* to Brian, he could use an <u>upright posture</u> to appear taller and more <u>powerful</u>. His steps could be <u>deliberately slow</u> to show that he wants to intimidate Brian.

3) To show his dominance, Phil could <u>stand close to Brian</u>, bring his face right up to Brian's and force <u>eye contact</u> with him. This would show that Phil is in <u>control</u> of the situation and hint at his <u>aggressive</u> side.

4) Phil could also use <u>physical contact</u> to intimidate Brian — the stage directions say he *"lays a hand on his shoulder"*, which may <u>prevent</u> Brian <u>moving away</u> from him. Phil could also put his finger to <u>Brian's lips</u> when he says "shhhh". This would mean that Brian <u>can't protest</u> vocally and would highlight that Phil is in <u>total control</u>.

Effect on the Audience

The more <u>threatening</u> Phil is in this scene, the more the audience will <u>sympathise</u> with Brian's eventual decision to go along with Phil's plan.

5) An actor playing Brian could <u>hunch</u> his body, <u>cower</u> and <u>look down</u> at his feet to show his fear. As Phil talks, Brian could <u>bite his lip</u> to suggest he's trying not to cry. He might <u>flinch</u> when Phil touches him to show he is afraid of Phil.

Sound Design — Sound Effects

Sound effects could be used to emphasise how real Phil's threats feel to Brian. For example, the sound of <u>rocks clinking</u> against metal could be made live off stage when Phil says "We'll throw rocks". When Phil says "You'll fall into the cold", a <u>recording</u> of a scream fading as if someone is falling could be used to reflect Brian's terror and add to the <u>uneasy mood</u>.

Leah talks to Phil about change

1) Leah's monologue at the end of Act Two offers many opportunities for <u>humour</u>. An actor's <u>vocal skills</u> are important in shaping how the audience <u>responds</u> to this scene.

2) To create humour, an actor playing Leah could convey her <u>excitement</u> about her moment of déjà vu by speaking <u>quickly</u>, <u>loudly</u> and at a <u>high pitch</u>. She could <u>stress</u> words like "exactly" and "knew" to show her <u>belief</u> in what she's saying. Her enthusiasm about something so innocent could be <u>amusing</u> for the audience.

Effect on the Audience

Leah's comment that she has "been here before" creates <u>dramatic irony</u> because of the repeated structure of the play. This could be <u>humorous</u> for the audience.

© Helen Murray / ArenaPAL

Leah has a hopeful facial expression as she waits for Phil to speak.

3) An actor could show Leah's growing <u>frustration</u> at Phil's silence when she <u>repeats</u> his name. The repetition of "Phil?" could initially be delivered in a <u>sing-song voice</u> to suggest she's asking <u>sweetly</u>, then with increasing <u>volume</u> and a harsher tone to reflect how annoyed she is — this could create <u>humour</u> for the audience.

4) The end of the monologue is more downbeat. Leah questions whether people have the <u>power</u> to "change things". She claims to believe they do, but an actor could use a <u>hesitant tone</u> to say "Well I do". This would make the audience <u>doubt</u> her claim, and hint that the group are doomed to continue making <u>bad decisions</u>.

EXAM TIP

You've probably heard my déjà vu joke before...

You should think about how all the elements of a production affect the audience's experience, from facial expressions to the use of sound effects. Make sure you're confident writing about all the different elements.

Act Three

Things only seem to get worse for the group in Act Three — Adam is found living in a hedge and Phil comes up with a plan to kill him so people don't find out the group lied. The games kids play these days...

Act Three ramps up the tension

1) The <u>tension</u> increases in Act Three as the characters are forced to make another tough decision. The act eventually reaches a <u>dramatic climax</u>, where the tension is at its <u>highest</u>.

2) Adam's return is the <u>driving force</u> behind the tension in this act. Cathy <u>explains</u> that she and Brian found Adam in a hedge and she threatened him to make him come out. At the same time, Brian shows signs of a <u>mental breakdown</u> by eating soil and babbling about irrelevant topics. The behaviour of these two characters will make the audience <u>uneasy</u>.

© Helen Murray / ArenaPAL

3) The tension rises when Adam tells his side of the story in a <u>disjointed</u> way — it is clear that he is <u>physically</u> and <u>mentally ill</u>. The group's decision to send Adam back to the hedge rather than help him builds tension further and creates <u>dread</u> about what will happen to Adam.

Effect on the Audience

In Act Three, the audience is likely to <u>feel sorry</u> for Adam. This will make Leah, who stands up for him, <u>more likeable</u>, and characters like Phil and Cathy, who opt to kill him, <u>less likeable</u>.

4) The <u>climax</u> arrives as Phil arranges Adam's murder. Leah's <u>realisation</u> dawns slowly, first as Phil sends other characters away and then as he gives vague instructions to Cathy and Brian. Leah tries and <u>fails</u> to stop the murder — her <u>helplessness</u> is frightening.

5) The tension is <u>lower</u> in the final scene of Act Three, when Leah <u>leaves</u> Phil. However, it is a powerful moment as it hints that their relationship is <u>damaged beyond repair</u>.

Cathy and Brian explain how they found Adam

Cathy grows <u>increasingly frustrated</u> at Brian's childlike mental state as they explain how they found Adam — actors could use <u>physical</u> and <u>vocal skills</u> to show the characters' feelings and relationship.

Physical Skills — Movement and Expression

- Cathy could <u>stand still</u> while Brian <u>bounces</u> around her. Brian's eccentric actions could <u>add humour</u>, but they would also highlight his <u>troubled</u> mental state.

- Brian could approach other characters with <u>open arms</u> and <u>grab</u> Cathy's hand when he says that everyone should "hold hands". This would <u>contrast</u> with his earlier <u>subdued</u> and <u>frightened</u> manner.

- An actor could show that Cathy is becoming <u>increasingly annoyed</u> with Brian by <u>frowning</u> or <u>rolling her eyes</u> every time he speaks. This could create <u>tension</u> as the audience would sense that Cathy is losing her patience.

- Cathy's irritation comes to a head when she "*slaps*" Brian — she could do this <u>without warning</u> and remain <u>expressionless</u> as she does it to make it more <u>shocking</u>.

Vocal Skills — Tone and Volume

- Cathy could deliver most of her lines in a <u>deadpan tone</u> to show a lack of emotion. She could use a <u>cheerful</u> tone when she talks about gouging Adam's eye out — this would make her sound more <u>sinister</u>.

- Cathy could speak <u>loudly</u> over Brian when she interrupts him. This would highlight her <u>irritation</u> with Brian, and suggest that she is pretending he is not there.

- An actor playing Brian could deliver his lines in an <u>excited tone</u> to reflect his new <u>lack of inhibitions</u>. He could also say lines like "I found him, I found him" in a <u>singsong</u> voice to make him seem like a <u>young child</u> — this may be disturbing for the audience.

Stage fighting needs to be safe — the actors should rehearse how to make the slap seem real without harming one another.

Act Three

Adam tells his side of the story

1) Adam's <u>monologue</u> shows that he is injured and mentally ill. An actor could use <u>vocal skills</u> to show Adam's damaged physical and mental state and create <u>unease</u> in the audience.

2) Adam's monologue is spread over numerous lines and filled with <u>pauses</u> and <u>ellipses</u>. These hesitations could be <u>drawn out</u> to suggest that Adam is having difficulty piecing events together. He could deliver the lines in a <u>weak tone</u> to show his fragile state — this would make the audience <u>sympathise</u> with him.

3) The <u>speed</u> of Adam's speech could vary. Parts such as "walking, crawling in this dark" could come out in a <u>rush</u> to show that remembering the fall <u>scares</u> him. He could <u>trail off</u> on other points to suggest he's reliving the experience — for example, when he says the light is "high, high...", he could speak <u>slowly</u> and let his voice <u>fade</u> to suggest he's picturing the light.

4) <u>Emphasis</u> could be placed on words like "dead" and "dark" to suggest Adam's <u>primal fear</u> of these things.

5) An actor could vary the <u>volume</u> of Adam's monologue to suggest <u>different emotions</u> — he could speak in a <u>quiet voice</u> to show fear, but he could <u>raise his voice</u> for lines like "I do know my name" to show that he feels the need to <u>defend himself</u> against the group.

Costume Design — Hair and Make-Up

- A designer could use make-up to make Adam's eyes look <u>red</u> and add <u>dark bags</u> underneath. This would make him appear <u>tired</u> and <u>ill</u>.

- The *"gash"* on Adam's forehead could be made to <u>stand out</u> by giving the actor <u>pale foundation</u> and using vivid <u>red make-up</u> for the injury. This sign of <u>physical injury</u> would make the audience more <u>sympathetic</u> towards him.

- The stage directions say Adam's hair is *"matted"*. A designer could use wax to make his hair look <u>tangled</u> and dark power to make it look <u>dirty</u>, showing that Adam isn't <u>taking care</u> of himself.

Leah realises that Phil intends to kill Adam

1) It's initially <u>unclear</u> to both Leah and the audience that Phil is planning Adam's murder. Leah's growing <u>realisation</u> and the way that Phil <u>cuts her out</u> of the discussion could be shown through <u>proxemics</u>.

2) Leah asks Phil "what are you doing?" when it becomes clear he doesn't plan to help Adam. She could stand in <u>close proximity</u> to Phil — this would show that she is <u>standing up</u> to him and that she is <u>determined</u> to change his mind.

3) When Phil talks to Cathy and Brian, he could <u>stand close</u> to them and <u>at a distance from Leah</u> so that she is alone — this would show she is <u>cut off</u> from the group. This would emphasise Phil's <u>control</u> — he is able to dictate who is in or out of the group.

4) When Cathy says "Yeah. I do." she could stand <u>right next</u> to Phil to highlight her <u>rising status</u> in the group.

5) At the end of the scene, Phil and Leah are the only characters on stage — they could stand at <u>opposite ends</u> of the stage to emphasise the <u>emotional distance</u> between them.

© Hull Truck Theatre

Effect on the Audience

The audience may <u>empathise</u> with Leah's helplessness because they also want to prevent Adam's death but are <u>unable</u> to do so.

EXAM TIP

What kind of person dies twice — A-dam unlucky one...

You can do a lot in Act Three to create different effects on the audience. Although you may have loads of good Ideas, it's important in the exam to keep your answer focused on answering the question.

Act Four

The group have successfully got away with murder by the time Act Four rolls around — hooray! But Leah has left, Phil is moping and the group is worse off than before. Maybe not hooray...

Act Four ends unhappily

1) Act Four leaves lots of issues <u>unresolved</u>, such as whether the postman is convicted and what Phil will do. However, the audience does learn that most of the characters have changed <u>for the worse</u> — this creates a <u>gloomy mood</u>.

2) Jan and Mark's language in their final duologue, as with previous duologues, is <u>vague</u>. This creates tension — the audience hopes to find out about <u>Adam</u> but instead learns that <u>Leah</u> has moved away.

3) The play ends with Richard trying to <u>convince</u> Phil to rejoin the group. Richard's <u>negative</u> descriptions of the other characters' lives, along with Phil's silence, creates a <u>sombre ending</u> to the play.

© Hull Truck Theatre

Jan and Mark talk about Leah moving away

There's little to suggest that Jan and Mark have been <u>greatly affected</u> by the events of the play. <u>Staging</u> could be used to reinforce this interpretation when they talk at the start of Act Four. For example:

1) On a <u>thrust stage</u>, Jan and Mark could stand <u>upstage</u>, far away from the apron. Their <u>distance</u> from the audience would emphasise their <u>detachment</u> from the rules and values of <u>society</u>.

2) If they stood <u>together</u> in the centre of a <u>large</u> performance space, it would emphasise their continuing <u>closeness</u> and hint that they are <u>united</u> against the rest of the world.

3) Staging the play <u>in the round</u> would mean that the characters were <u>surrounded</u> by the audience. This could give the sense that society is <u>watching</u> them, hinting that their <u>secrets</u> may not remain <u>hidden</u> for long.

Costume Design — Clothing and Hair

Jan and Mark's clothes and hair styles in this scene could be just as <u>neat</u> and <u>fashionable</u> as <u>earlier</u> in the play — this would communicate that their lives have continued as <u>normal</u>.

Richard explains what everyone is doing

1) Richard's description of what's happening shows the <u>impact</u> of the play's events on the group. An actor playing Richard could use <u>vocal skills</u> to create a sense of <u>hopelessness</u> in their futures.

2) Richard could <u>stress</u> words like "insane" and "hates". This would emphasise the <u>negativity</u> of the characters' lives and create a <u>mood of despair</u>.

3) He could use a <u>worried tone</u> to say "I feel sorry for Lou" — this would suggest to the audience that things may continue to <u>get worse</u> for the characters.

4) Questions like "Aren't you interested?" could be delivered in a <u>loud voice</u> to indicate Richard's <u>annoyance</u> at Phil's lack of reaction. Richard's final line, "Phil?", could be delivered in an <u>uncertain</u>, <u>trembling</u> voice to highlight his <u>concern</u> and create a <u>downbeat ending</u>.

Sound Design — Underscoring

<u>Sombre music</u> could fade in as Richard says "You can't stay here forever" and continue until the end of the play. This would enhance the <u>mournful mood</u>.

EXAM TIP

This ending is too sour for even Phil to digest...

Writing about how to direct, perform and design some parts of the play will be harder than others. Don't panic — there are no right or wrong suggestions. Just explain the reasons behind each of your choices.

Practice Questions

I imagine you're feeling a lot closer to the play after all of that close analysis. The best way to show how much you've taken in is by trying these questions — remember to write a paragraph or so for the in-depth ones.

Quick Questions

1) What kind of mood might a director aim to create in Act One?

2) Suggest one way a costume designer could show that Brian is an outsider.

3) Why might a lighting designer choose to use red-tinted gels when Leah attempts to strangle herself in Act One?

4) Give two examples of diegetic sounds that might be used in Act Two ("*A Wood*").

5) Why might an actor playing Phil use physical contact when threatening Brian in Act Two?

6) How might an actor show Leah's excitement about her déjà vu in Act Two?

7) Why might a costume designer choose to make the wound on Adam's head stand out?

8) What effect would be created by Leah standing at a distance from Phil at the end of Act Three ("*A Wood*")?

9) Give one way an actor playing Richard might use vocal skills to create a mood of despair in Act Four.

In-depth Questions

1) Describe a set design for the street in Act One, then explain how this set would change in Act Four. Explain the effect of these changes on the audience.

2) In Act One ("*A Wood*"), Jan and Mark describe what happened to Adam. How might the actor playing Jan use vocal skills to reveal information about her character here?

3) Choose a moment from Act Two. Explain how sound could be used to create a particular atmosphere at this moment.

4) How could an actor playing Leah use physical skills to help create a climax to the tension at the end of Act Three ("*A Wood*")?

5) Explain how lighting could be used to create a bleak mood in Act Four ("*A Field*").

Practice Questions

This is it, the last set of exam-style questions. By now you should be a DNA expert, so pull on your lab coat and get that microscope ready. (Wait, sorry, wrong revision guide.) To practise what you've learnt about the play (not about the molecules that carry genetic information), write some smashing answers to the questions below.

Exam-style Questions

> Read Act One ("*A Wood*") from where Mark says "**It's Adam. He's...**" to where John Tate says "**Dead. He's dead**", then answer Questions 1 and 2 below.

1) As a sound designer working on a production of *DNA*, describe how you would use sound to enhance the production of this extract.

2) Discuss how a performer playing Mark could communicate key aspects of his character to the audience in this extract. You should consider Mark's motivations and how the actor could use vocal and physical skills.

> Read Act Three ("*A Field*") from the stage direction "***PHIL sits with a bag***" to "***Irritated he puts it carefully away***", then answer Questions 3 and 4.

3) As a performer playing the role of Phil, discuss how you would use physical skills to portray him in this extract. You should explain why your ideas are suitable for this extract and for the play as a whole.

4) Imagine you are a designer working on *DNA*. Explain how you would use props and stage furniture to portray this extract effectively on stage to the audience. You should refer to the play's context in your answer.

> Read Act Three ("*A Wood*") from where Leah says "**What happened**" to where Adam says "**I'm... dead?**", then answer Question 5.

5) Imagine you are a director creating a production of *DNA*. Discuss how the performer playing Adam might convey Adam's state of mind in this extract. You should consider the performer's use of physical skills, vocal skills and stage space.

About the Exam

If you're reading this book, you're going to write about *DNA* in your exam. Thankfully, this section is full of brilliant exam tips and sample answers to help you prepare for the big day. Take a deep breath and read on...

'DNA' will be assessed in a written exam

1) One section of your exam will require you to answer questions on *DNA*. The questions will either focus on an <u>extract</u>, or an extract <u>and</u> the play <u>as a whole</u>. In some cases, you can <u>choose</u> an extract <u>yourself</u>.

2) For this part of the exam, you'll be <u>assessed</u> on your <u>knowledge</u> of <u>how</u> the play could be <u>produced</u> and <u>performed</u>.

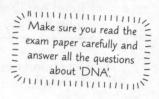
Make sure you read the exam paper carefully and answer all the questions about 'DNA'.

3) There will be both <u>short-answer</u> and <u>long-answer questions</u>. Manage your <u>time carefully</u> so you have <u>plenty of time</u> to write the longer answers — if a question is worth <u>twice the marks</u> of another, you should spend <u>twice as long</u> on it.

You'll have to come up with ideas of how to produce 'DNA'

1) The questions could ask you to write about how a <u>performer</u>, <u>designer</u> or <u>director</u> may do something:

- You'll need to think about how a **PERFORMER** might use performance skills to portray a certain <u>character</u>. This could include <u>physical skills</u> and <u>vocal skills</u>.
- You'll need to come up with **DESIGN** ideas that would enhance the impact of the <u>play</u>. This requires a good <u>understanding</u> of design elements like <u>set</u>, <u>lighting</u> and <u>sound</u>.
- You'll need to consider how a **DIRECTOR** would bring the <u>written text</u> to life <u>on stage</u>. You'll be asked to focus on <u>one element</u> of the <u>production</u> in your answer.

2) Some questions <u>tell</u> you which aspects of performance or design to write about, or you might be allowed to <u>choose</u>. You may be given <u>options</u> to choose from — e.g. <u>set</u>, <u>lighting</u> or <u>sound</u>.

3) You <u>can't</u> just learn about the roles and responsibilities of <u>one type</u> of theatre maker — over the course of the written exam, you might be expected to answer questions about <u>all three aspects of production</u>.

You'll always need to write about certain aspects

1) No matter which aspect you're writing about, there are some <u>general points</u> you'll need to <u>consider</u>:

- Kelly's <u>intentions</u> and what he wants to convey — <u>stage directions</u> are useful for this.
- How the play's <u>historical</u>, <u>social</u>, <u>cultural</u> and <u>theatrical contexts</u> might <u>affect</u> a production.
- The <u>roles</u> and <u>responsibilities</u> of <u>theatre makers</u> and how they bring the play to life, as well as any <u>challenges</u> they may face.
- The <u>genre</u> and <u>style</u> of the play. You should explore how these can be <u>conveyed</u> to the <u>audience</u>.
- The <u>desired effect</u> of a production on the <u>audience</u>, as well as <u>how</u> this effect might be <u>created</u>.

2) To get <u>top marks</u> in the exam, you should <u>also</u>:

- Use accurate <u>technical language</u> when describing <u>performance skills</u> and <u>design features</u>.
- Use <u>examples</u> (e.g. <u>quotes</u> and <u>context</u>) to show <u>understanding</u> of the play and <u>support</u> your points.
- Give <u>specific</u>, <u>detailed</u> suggestions on <u>how</u> you could <u>perform</u>, <u>design</u> or <u>direct</u> a production — this will help the examiner to <u>visualise</u> your ideas.

About the Exam

Read the extract carefully before you begin

If you're sitting the Eduqas exam, the question might also ask you to <u>choose</u> a scene from the play to write about.

1) Most of the exam questions about *DNA* will ask you to refer to an <u>extract</u>, so make sure you've <u>fully understood</u> it before you start writing.

2) Some questions will also ask you to write about the <u>play as a whole</u>, so you'll need to <u>relate your ideas</u> about how to stage the extract to other <u>ideas</u> or <u>events</u> in the play.

3) Read each question <u>carefully</u>, then read through the extract. Think about what happens <u>before</u> and <u>after</u> the extract to help you work out how it <u>fits in</u> with the <u>rest</u> of the play. <u>Highlight</u> any <u>important words</u> or <u>phrases</u> (including <u>stage directions</u>). You might also want to <u>annotate</u> the extract as you go along.

4) For <u>shorter answers</u>, you should start writing as soon as you feel <u>comfortable</u> with the extract. But for <u>longer answers</u>, you should <u>plan</u> out a few key <u>ideas</u> for your answers. You could do this by jotting down some <u>bullet points</u> or making a quick <u>diagram</u> (see p.68).

5) Your answer should be <u>coherent</u> — not just a list of <u>different</u> possibilities for the extract. For example, if you start writing about a naturalistic approach, don't <u>swap</u> to a non-naturalistic one <u>halfway through</u>. A good <u>plan</u> will help to make sure your ideas <u>flow</u> and are <u>well-structured</u>.

Shorter answers should be concise

Remember that you shouldn't spend too much time on <u>short-answer</u> questions that aren't worth many marks — your <u>answers</u> will need to be <u>snappy</u> and <u>straight to the point</u>. Have a look at this example:

> Imagine you are playing Richard in a production of *DNA*.
> Give three examples of physical skills that you would use to portray Richard in Act One ("*A Wood*"). Give reasons for your suggestions.

Turn to p.68-71 for examples of what a longer question and answer might look like.

The first sentence <u>directly addresses</u> the question.

At the start of Act One ("*A Wood*"), when Richard stands up to John Tate, I would stand very upright, raise my chin and clench my fists. This would make Richard look defiant. However, the stage directions state that Richard moves towards John Tate "*a little hesitantly*", so I would move slowly and drag my feet slightly. This would communicate Richard's wariness of John Tate to the audience. John Tate responds aggressively to Richard's resistance, which causes Richard to back down. At this point, I would bow my head and avoid eye contact with John Tate when he says "Have you got a side now, Richard?" This would make Richard seem submissive.

The answer refers to <u>precise</u> moments in the extract.

Every suggestion should be <u>clearly explained</u> to the examiner.

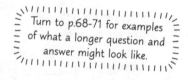

Manage your time carefully in the exam...

The questions will be worth different marks in the exam. Make sure you don't spend all your time on questions that are worth fewer marks — plan ahead for roughly how long you should spend on each one.

Sample Question and Answer

For the higher-mark questions in the exam, you'll have to write longer answers and explain your ideas in plenty of detail. These two pages show you what an exam answer about performance might look like.

Here's a sample question about performance

Here's what a long question about <u>performance</u> might look like:

> Find the part of Act Two where Leah talks to Phil about happiness. Read from where Leah says "**Are you happy?**" to where she says "**What have we done, Phil?**", then answer the question below.
>
> Imagine you're playing Leah in a production of *DNA*. As a performer, discuss how you might convey key aspects of Leah's character to the audience in this extract and the play as a whole. You should consider physical skills, vocal skills and interactions with other characters.

If you're sitting the Edexcel exam, the extract will be printed in your exam paper. If you're sitting the Eduqas exam, you'll be told which pages to read from your copy of the play.

Here's how you could plan your answer...

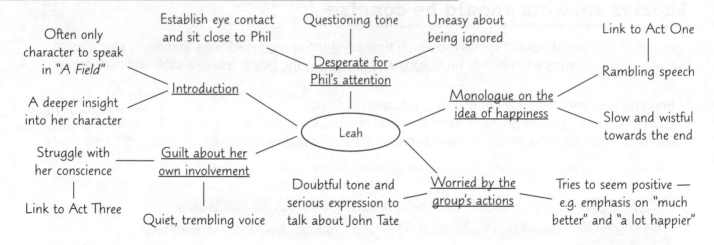

Often only character to speak in "A Field"

A deeper insight into her character

Establish eye contact and sit close to Phil

Questioning tone

Uneasy about being ignored

Desperate for Phil's attention

Introduction

Leah

Struggle with her conscience

Link to Act Three

Guilt about her own involvement

Quiet, trembling voice

Doubtful tone and serious expression to talk about John Tate

Worried by the group's actions

Monologue on the idea of happiness

Link to Act One

Rambling speech

Slow and wistful towards the end

Tries to seem positive — e.g. emphasis on "much better" and "a lot happier"

... and here's how you could write it

Keep your introduction <u>brief</u> and focused on the <u>question</u>.

The scenes that take place in "A Field" provide the audience with an insight into Leah's character, because she's usually the only person to speak. In this extract, Leah's monologue reveals several key aspects of her character, including her feelings about Phil, her anxiety about the group's actions and her sense of guilt.

This picks out <u>one aspect</u> of the <u>character</u> and explains how it might be <u>performed</u>.

Throughout the whole extract, I would choose to show that Leah is desperate for Phil's attention. I would convey this to the audience by sitting in close proximity to Phil and trying to make eye contact with him at key moments. I would speak with rising intonation at the end of lines like "Isn't it Phil? Phil?" to give Leah's speech a questioning tone. This would make it seem like she is inviting Phil to respond. However, Leah feels uneasy when Phil doesn't reply to her, which I would reflect using body language. I would sit cross-legged on the stage, but keep shuffling around to suggest that Leah is unable to make herself comfortable. The stage directions state that Leah is holding a *"container"*, so I would also drum my fingers on it nervously.

You can quote <u>stage directions</u>, but you should add your <u>own ideas</u> to them.

Section Six — Exam Advice

Sample Question and Answer

Leah's visible anxiety would encourage the audience to feel sympathy for her, as well as drawing their attention to this important prop.

> This considers the impact of your decisions on the audience.

Leah starts her monologue by discussing the idea of happiness. Her speech at this point is somewhat garbled, so I would speak at a quick pace and only pause for breath occasionally to create the impression that Leah is rambling about the first thing that comes to mind. In Act One, she is similarly incoherent when she obsesses over Phil's opinion of her. As a result, my delivery of the Act Two extract would reinforce the audience's impression of Leah as a character who is prone to overthinking. In contrast, I would speak slowly and use a wistful tone of voice when Leah starts talking about the "happiest moment" in her life, as well as breaking eye contact with Phil and staring into the distance. This would suggest to the audience that Leah is picturing a simpler time before Adam's disappearance and wishing that she could go back to it, hinting that she already regrets the cover-up.

> Explain how your choices relate to the rest of the play.

> Use short quotes to show which part of the extract you're referring to.

Leah's update on the other characters suggests that she wants to convince herself that their actions were justified. When she claims that "Everyone's happier" since Adam's disappearance, I would add emphasis to phrases like "much better" and "a lot happier", to show her determination to believe that their situation has improved. I would also use a wide-eyed facial expression and a disbelieving tone of voice to say that Danny and Cathy are behaving like "old friends", as though Leah inwardly doubts that such changes are genuine. Leah's revelation that John Tate "won't come out of his room" casts further doubt on the idea that life has really improved for the group. To reflect this, I would pause for a long time before mentioning John Tate and use a serious facial expression. This would make Leah seem more doubtful and reinforce the sense that she was only speaking about the rest of the group in order to convince herself that their decision to cover up Adam's disappearance was acceptable.

> The question asks you to write about physical and vocal skills.

> Describe how the performance develops as the extract goes on.

At the end of the extract, it becomes even clearer to the audience that Leah feels guilty about the group's treatment of Adam. When she reveals that "Adam's parents were on the telly again last night", I would speak in a quiet, trembling voice to show that she is upset and afraid. I would also use regular phrasing to provide a contrast to Leah's babbled speech earlier in the extract. This would add further to the audience's impression that she is now being serious. When Phil "looks up", I would look at him hopefully, as though Leah expects him to show some sign of guilt that would indicate that he isn't as remorseless as she fears. However, I would hang my head and sag my shoulders when she realises that Phil is staying quiet, before saying "What have we done, Phil?" in a desperate tone. This would emphasise to the audience that Leah is struggling with her conscience. The audience may even interpret this as an early sign that she's losing patience with Phil and the rest of the group, foreshadowing her departure at the end of Act Three.

> Don't forget to say how you'd interact with the other performers.

> This shows good awareness of the play as a whole.

EXAM TIP

I'll bet Phil didn't get full marks in his speaking exam...

With the longer questions, it's tempting to write down every single idea you have, but this can make your answer pretty messy. Instead, make sure that all your points are relevant to what the question is asking.

Section Six — Exam Advice

Sample Question and Answer

You'll need to write about design as well as performance in your exam, so here's a sample answer that does just that. This answer takes the same extract as before and looks at it from the perspective of a designer.

Here's a sample question about design

Here's what a long question about <u>design</u> might look like:

> Find the part of Act Two where Leah talks to Phil about happiness. Read from where Leah says "**Are you happy?**" to where she says "**What have we done, Phil?**", then answer the question below.
>
> Imagine you're a designer working on a production of *DNA*. Discuss how you would use **either** set design, lighting **or** sound to stage this extract effectively for the audience.

This question asks you to choose one design element, but you may be asked to write about multiple elements in the same answer if you're sitting the Eduqas exam.

Here's how you could plan your answer...

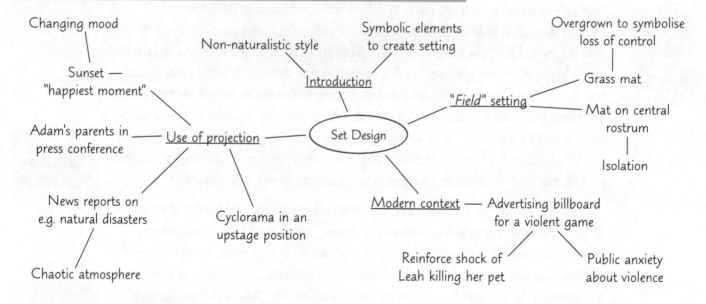

Changing mood

Sunset — "happiest moment"

Adam's parents in press conference — Use of projection

News reports on e.g. natural disasters

Chaotic atmosphere

Cyclorama in an upstage position

Non-naturalistic style

Symbolic elements to create setting

Introduction

Set Design

"*Field*" setting — Overgrown to symbolise loss of control

Grass mat

Mat on central rostrum

Isolation

Modern context — Advertising billboard for a violent game

Reinforce shock of Leah killing her pet

Public anxiety about violence

... and here's how you could write it

Use the introduction to describe the <u>overall effect</u> you want to create.

When staging this extract, I would use symbolic elements to establish the setting and context of the extract. These elements would form part of a non-naturalistic style that would enhance the mood and atmosphere of the extract. The design would also highlight some of the key issues raised in the extract, including the nature of happiness, environmental change and public anxiety about violence among young people.

This extract is set in "A Field", so I would use an artificial grass mat to convey this setting. The grass would be longer and more ragged than in Act One; only "four days" have passed since the events of Act One, so this unnaturally rapid growth would symbolise the way that events are spiralling out of the group's control at this point in the play.

This <u>describes</u> the set design and <u>justifies</u> your choices.

Section Six — Exam Advice

Sample Question and Answer

It's important to say where each element of your design goes on stage.

Leah's monologue about happiness creates a sense of isolation, so I would place the grass mat at a higher level to the rest of the stage using a centre stage rostrum to symbolise Leah and Phil's separation from society. This would enhance the impact of Leah's monologue about the loneliness of "pretending to be happy". I would further this effect by making the rostrum only just large enough for the two actors to sit on; this would mean that it was surrounded by lots of empty stage space, which would add to the impression that Leah and Phil are separated from the rest of the group and from society as a whole. This would add to the mood of loneliness.

As well as giving the audience a sense of place and enhancing the mood of the extract, my set design would reflect the play's 21st-century setting. To achieve this effect, I would paint a truck to look like a modern advertising billboard, which would be easy to wheel on and off stage. This would be placed in a upstage right position and on a lower level to Leah and Phil, so that the audience's focus remains on the characters. One of the most shocking moments of the extract is Leah's revelation that she killed her pet; to reinforce the violence of her action, the billboard would show an advert for a violent video game. This would remind the audience of public anxiety about violence among young people, prompting them to think more deeply about the answer to Leah's question, "Why do you think I did that?"

This shows an understanding of the context.

This shows that you've considered some of the play's wider messages.

Having established the setting and context, I would use projection to enhance the impact of important moments during Leah's monologue. For example, I would project a silent montage of news reports about climate change and natural disasters on a cyclorama behind the actors when Leah talks about "polluting the natural order". These rapidly changing images would create a chaotic atmosphere and add to the sense of anxiety created by Leah's concerns about the "fragility of reality". I would use the projector again when Leah says that Adam's parents were "on the telly". At this point, I would show a video in the style of a press conference with two actors playing Adam's parents grieving and appealing for information. This would suggest that Leah saw this clip on television and cannot get it out of her mind, which would emphasise her guilty conscience to the audience.

Explain your design ideas using accurate technical terms.

Use quotes to indicate when certain effects would be used.

Always refer back to the effect on the audience.

I would also use projection to change the atmosphere of the scene. For example, the mood briefly becomes lighter when Leah talks about her "happiest moment". At this point, I would project a still image of the sun setting over a generic town onto the cyclorama. The warm oranges and pinks would reflect Leah's happiness as she remembers the moment, and use colour symbolism to create a sense of romance. When Phil doesn't respond to Leah's question about whether he remembers the sunset, the screen would abruptly go black to reflect her sense of disappointment. This would also emphasise the bleak mood created by Leah's next sentence: her admission that she has killed her pet.

Show that you've thought about the whole extract.

EXAM TIP

I assume Leah's got a separate container for her lunch...

When you're writing about design, it's important to give lots of detail in your answers. Clearly explain how you'd achieve the effects you want and use technical terms when describing what you would do.

Glossary

backstory	The events that have happened to a character <u>before</u> the action of the play.
blackout	When the <u>stage lights</u> are <u>turned off</u> between scenes or at the end of a performance.
blocking	The process of <u>positioning</u> the actors on stage and planning their <u>movements</u> to maintain <u>good sightlines</u> for the <u>audience</u>.
body language	The way <u>movements</u>, <u>posture</u> and <u>gestures</u> can show how someone feels <u>without speaking</u>.
'Broken Britain'	A phrase used by the media and politicians in the early 21st century to describe a British society in which people acted for <u>themselves</u> rather than in a <u>socially responsible</u> way.
character arc	The way a character <u>changes</u> over the course of a story.
climax	The <u>turning point</u> in a play, where <u>tension</u> is at its <u>highest</u>.
comedy	A genre of drama which features <u>humour</u> and a <u>happy ending</u>.
convention	A feature of <u>staging</u>, <u>design</u> or <u>performance</u> that is associated with a particular style or time.
cyclorama	A <u>curved screen</u> at the back of the stage which can have scenery <u>projected</u> onto it.
déjà vu	The feeling of having <u>done</u> or <u>seen</u> something <u>before</u>.
diction	The <u>quality</u> (or clarity) of a performer's <u>vocal expression</u>.
diegetic sound	A sound that <u>can be heard</u> by the <u>characters</u> in a play.
DNA	A complex <u>chemical</u> found in all living organisms. It carries <u>genetic information</u>.
dramatic irony	When the audience <u>knows</u> something that the characters <u>don't</u>.
duologue	A <u>scene</u> or <u>section of dialogue</u> which only involves <u>two actors</u>.
end-on stage	A <u>proscenium arch</u> stage <u>without</u> the <u>arch</u> to frame it.
flat	A <u>wooden frame</u> with <u>canvas</u> stretched over it which is <u>painted</u> and used as <u>scenery</u>.
floodlight	A type of stage lantern which casts a <u>broad</u> wash of light onto the stage.
fourth wall	The <u>imaginary barrier</u> that separates the <u>audience</u> from the world of the play <u>on stage</u>.
Fresnel spotlight	A type of stage lantern which casts a <u>beam</u> with a <u>softly defined edge</u>.
gel	A piece of <u>coloured</u>, <u>heat-resistant</u>, <u>plastic film</u> used to <u>change</u> the <u>colour</u> of a lantern's <u>beam</u>.
genre	The <u>type of story</u> a play is telling (e.g. <u>comedy</u>, <u>tragedy</u>).
gesture	A <u>movement</u> made by <u>part of the body</u> (e.g. arms, head) to convey a character's <u>emotions</u>.
gobo	A <u>thin</u>, <u>metal disc</u> with <u>shapes</u> cut into it which can be slotted into a lantern to <u>project patterns</u> or <u>images</u> onto the <u>stage</u> or a <u>backdrop</u>.
incidental music	Any <u>music</u> which <u>accompanies</u> a performance and is used to create <u>mood</u> or <u>tension</u>.
intonation	The <u>rise</u> and <u>fall</u> of a performer's <u>voice</u> to create a <u>natural</u> pattern of speech.
in-yer-face theatre	A genre of theatre which uses <u>shocking</u> or <u>violent</u> means to convey a <u>serious message</u>.
lighting rig	A <u>structure</u> above the stage and wings which <u>holds</u> the <u>stage lanterns</u>.
linear structure	A plot structure where the events on stage happen in <u>chronological order</u>.
minimalist set	A <u>basic set</u> that uses <u>minimal</u> scenery and <u>very few</u> props.

Glossary

monologue	A speech made by one character, either to another character or to the audience.
naturalism	A style of theatre which tries to recreate real life on stage as closely as possible.
non-diegetic sound	A sound that can't be heard by the characters in the play.
parcan	A stage lantern that can produce an intense and adjustable beam.
phrasing	The way a character's dialogue is broken up into sections when spoken by an actor.
physical theatre	A non-naturalistic style of theatre which uses physical movements to tell stories.
plot device	Something (or someone) that is only included in the play to move the plot forward.
posture	The position a character holds themselves in when sitting or standing.
profile spotlight	A type of stage lantern that produces a sharply defined beam. These lanterns are used to focus on a particular character or part of the stage.
promenade theatre	A style of theatre that requires the audience to follow the actors between different performance spaces over the course of the play. This usually takes place outdoors.
prop	An item on stage that the characters can interact with.
proscenium arch stage	A box-shaped stage that is set back from the audience so that only the front end is open to them..
proxemics	The use of the physical space between the actors on stage to create meaning.
revolving stage	A stage or part of a stage which can spin around.
rostrum (plural rostra)	A raised platform which is used to introduce different levels to the stage.
soundscape	A collection of individual sounds that are layered up to create a strong sense of place.
split staging	When the stage is split into different areas representing different places or times.
stage directions	Any instructions written in a script by the playwright to explain how a play should be performed.
stage furniture	Any moveable object on stage which isn't a costume, a prop or a part of the scenery.
strobe	A type of stage lantern which rapidly flashes on and off.
structure	The shape of a play's narrative, including the order in which it's shown to the audience.
style	The way in which a director chooses to interpret a performance text on stage.
symbolism	The use of props, gestures, setting, lighting, etc. to represent other things and create meaning.
tableau	A moment in a performance when the action stops and the characters freeze in position.
theatre in the round	A style of staging which seats the audience on all sides of a central stage.
thrust stage	A stage which extends out into the audience, so that they're standing or sitting on three sides.
tragedy	A genre of play which features a serious plot and an unhappy ending.
traverse stage	A long, narrow stage which runs between the audience, who face the stage on both sides.
truck	A structure on wheels which can be painted on both sides and used as scenery.
uplighting	When the stage is lit from below to create an unusual or unsettling effect.
wings	The space to the side of a stage which is used for storage and as a waiting area for the actors.

Index

The Characters in 'DNA'

Look at this lovely bunch. You should be familiar with them and the play by now, but if you want a recap, read on for the critically acclaimed *DNA — The Cartoon*. (Probably not coming to cinemas anytime soon).

Leah

Phil

Adam

After the bullying

Cathy

Brian

Richard

John Tate

Jan and Mark

Lou

Danny

Dennis Kelly's 'DNA'